PRAISE FOR *THIS IS AWKWARD*

"*This Is Awkward* reminds me that the grace of God goes far and deep, that His love does not leave us where it found us, and that there is freedom found just on the other side of facing up to our fear."

—Bob Goff, New York Times bestselling
author of Love Does

"Sammy Rhodes is funny, talented, and has an amazing story to tell."

—Jon Acuff, New York Times bestselling
author of Start and Do Over

"Sammy Rhodes is an imaginative, thoughtful, substantive, and funny voice. . . . Few people out there can combine deep wisdom with thoughtful hilarity. Sammy Rhodes does."

—Russell D. Moore, president of the
Ethics and Religious Liberty Commission,
Southern Baptist Convention

"With characteristic humor and endearing transparency, Sammy has helped me to feel less alone in the world. In this beautiful and courageous book, he revisits some of the most 'awkward' and painful chapters of his own story—but without a shred of self-indulgence. Instead, his words are an invitation for fellow strugglers to find rest, hope, and even laughter in the awkwardness that is our lives. Do yourself a favor and read this book. It has the potential to change your life."

—Scott Sauls, pastor and author of Jesus
Outside the Lines: A Way Forward for
Those Who Are Tired of Taking Sides

"Sammy Rhodes's hilarious book will give a lot of Christians permission to talk a lot more frankly about the sometimes-funny, often-devastating ways we hurt ourselves and others. Even better, it gives us confidence that those things can open a door to knowing and sharing God's love in ways we never thought possible."

—WESLEY HILL, ASSISTANT PROFESSOR OF
BIBLICAL STUDIES, TRINITY SCHOOL FOR
MINISTRY, AMBRIDGE, PENNSYLVANIA

THIS IS
AWKWARD

THIS IS AWKWARD

How Life's Uncomfortable Moments Open
the Door to Intimacy and Connection

Sammy Rhodes

NELSON
BOOKS

An Imprint of Thomas Nelson

Published in Nashville, Tennessee, by Nelson Books, an imprint of Thomas Nelson. Nelson Books and Thomas Nelson are registered trademarks of HarperCollins Christian Publishing, Inc.

Published in association with the literary agency of Wolgemuth & Associates, Inc.

Thomas Nelson titles may be purchased in bulk for educational, business, fund-raising, or sales promotional use. For information, please e-mail SpecialMarkets@ThomasNelson.com.

Library of Congress Cataloging-in-Publication Data

Names: Rhodes, Sammy, 1980-
Title: This is awkward : how life's uncomfortable moments open the door to intimacy and connection / Sammy Rhodes.
Description: Nashville : Thomas Nelson, 2016. | Includes bibliographical references.
Identifiers: LCCN 2015021446 | ISBN 9780718034931
Subjects: LCSH: Interpersonal relations--Religious aspects--Christianity. |Introversion--Religious aspects--Christianity. | Personality—Religious aspects--Christianity. | Emotions--Religious aspects--Christianity. | Self-consciousness (Sensitivity) | Embarrassment.
Classification: LCC BV4597.52 .R46 2016 | DDC 248.4--dc23
LC record available at http://lccn.loc.gov/2015021446

Printed in the United States of America
16 17 18 19 20 RRD 6 5 4 3 2 1

To my wife, Alyssa. Thank you for seeing all of my awkward and loving me. Also, I'm sorry about that time I cried and yelled at you for not reading my blogs.

CONTENTS

Introduction xi

Chapter 1: Don't Waste Your Awkwardness. 1

Chapter 2: Parents Are a Gift
(You Can't Return Them) 13

Chapter 3: *D* Is for Divorce 33

Chapter 4: The Porn in My Side. 47

Chapter 5: *D* Is Also for Depression 69

Chapter 6: I Kissed Marriage Hello After Kissing
Dating Goodbye 89

Chapter 7: Where Friendship Is Born 111

Chapter 8: Calling All Introverts
(They Probably Won't Pick Up) 127

Chapter 9: Donuts Are a Whole Food If
You Take Out the *W* 139

Chapter 10: Tweeting Ourselves to Death 155

Chapter 11: Side-Hugging Jesus 169

Acknowledgments 183

Appendix A: An Introvert's Guide to
Surviving a Party 187

Appendix B: A Social Media Manifesto 191

Notes. 195

About the Author 205

INTRODUCTION

Vulnerability Is Hard, but Grace Is True, So Let's Make Some Awkward

I 've always considered myself an awkward person. I can't tell you the first time I had this realization. It probably was a social situation that involved small talk. If I could have any superpower, it would be the ability to do small talk well, because anyone who does it well is a superhero as far as I'm concerned. I'm more like the Aquaman of small talk: people don't remember much about me except that I'm weird.

The feeling that I was awkward only increased when I got into ministry, a job that requires a good amount of social skills. When I first arrived at the University of South Carolina to take the position of RUF Campus Minister, the students in our ministry had two standing weekly traditions that made my awkwardness shine. One was called "stump the chump," where a group of six to eight students would meet me for lunch on campus so they could ask any burning questions that they had.

The other was sand volleyball. The game is straightforward enough, except that you've never seen me play sand volleyball. John Updike wrote, "Looking foolish does the spirit good."[1] I think God gave us sand volleyball for that very reason. Some of us are less like Goose and Maverick in *Top Gun* and more like the guys in the control center we never got to see play sand volleyball because it would have been too painful to watch.

I learned a lot about my awkwardness that first year at the university. I also learned that it's objectively weird to sit Indian style next to a sand volleyball court and just watch, especially when you have a mustache.

One of the perks of being awkward is that because people generally don't love being around you, you have plenty of time to think and write. This book is living proof. I hope that it's proof, too, that our awkward moments matter.

I can think of so many reasons I shouldn't write this book, though—sixteen to be exact:

1. Who am I to write a book? My experience consists almost entirely of writing things for the Internet: tweets, blog posts, and short articles. I feel like the e-cigarette version of a writer: not real and kind of annoying.
2. I was accused of plagiarism. An experiment in chasing Internet fame ended in conviction, a lifetime sentence of Internet infamy. What happens on the Internet stays

on the Internet. A quick Google search of my name should do the trick if you don't know the story. Google at your own risk. Apparently there is a certain kind of celebrity who bears a similar name.

3. My family might disown me. Anne Lamott once wrote, "You own everything that happened to you. Tell your stories. If people wanted you to write warmly about them, they should've behaved better."[2] I love my family and friends. I love my relationships with them. We've all come a long way, and I wouldn't be the person I am apart from them. Also, some of them should have behaved better. Mainly me.

4. I don't want to stir up Twittergate 2.0. I hope that I've learned from my mistakes. I've owned as much as I can and reached out to make amends where I thought it would be appropriate. But I would love not to stir up anything again.

5. I'm terrified of doing a book that is essentially a literary "selfie." The goal is to share my story where I believe it will be helpful. I pray it's not a bunch of narcissistic psychobabble.

6. I'm terrified of doing a book that is frowned upon by my tribe. The people and leaders in my particular corner of the Christian faith all mean the world to me, and I want to write something that makes them proud. I'm nervous this won't be the case.

7. I don't have a decent picture to go on the back of this book. No one tells you how weird it feels to ask a photographer to take your headshot. I completely understand

the people who used to think that having your picture taken steals a little part of your soul. Maybe I'll just use the caricature I had drawn for twenty dollars in Myrtle Beach when I was in the seventh grade.

8. I'm pretty awkward when signing autographs. It's happened a handful of times. Signing an autograph feels like using the bathroom at a football stadium: it's uncomfortable, dirty, and you hope no one sees you. Also, what do you write? From now on I'm just going to write, "This is awkward," because I mean it and it fits.

9. I wanted to do a book on donuts. It would have been an e-book consisting mainly of short reviews of the best donuts I've ever had. Maybe this dream will be book number three, after *The Fault in Our Starburst: A Brief History of the Yellow Ones*.

10. I don't have an author's name. Sammy? I've only seen my name in kids' books. My full name, Samuel, isn't any better. It sounds like I should have died fighting in the Civil War. Maybe I'll go with S. R. R. Rhodes. Seems to work for J. R. R. Tolkien and George R. R. Martin.

11. I don't have a cool soundtrack that helped me write this book. Unless you count the sounds coming from the ladies' parlor in the church where my office is, or the restless whines of our four children. I'm just going to claim The National. During most of my time writing, I half-listened to them. Also their music is mostly about feeling awkward and being vulnerable.

12. Who am I to tell my story? I know this is the voice of my insecurities talking. Also Satan. They sound a lot

alike. The courage to do so comes from the belief that my story matters to God and will be helpful to others. Because of that it is worth telling. Yours is too. I hope telling mine is an invitation for others to share in turn.

13. I didn't scribble my book on napkins while riding a train like J. K. Rowling. At least that's how I heard she wrote the first Harry Potter book. Mine has been hashed out on a MacBook Air in various coffee shops across town, which feels like a giant cliché. On the plus side, unlike J. K. Rowling, I can text "jk" to my friends to say I'm "just kidding" without confusing them.

14. I can't bring myself to call myself a writer. Maybe this will change, but it feels like the kind of bragging that makes everyone else roll their eyes. Calling yourself a writer feels like being the guy who brings a guitar to a party. You're shoving your perceived ability in everyone's faces. Maybe this will change when my donut e-book is a *New York Times* bestseller.

15. I don't smoke. Let me rephrase that. I don't smoke like real smokers smoke. Will I fake inhale an American Spirit with friends during a night out? Absolutely. Do my friends know I'm fake inhaling? Absolutely not. At least not until this very moment.

16. My insecurity runs deep. My greatest fear in writing a book is that it will be bad. My next greatest fear is that it will be boring. My next, next greatest fear is that the combination of these two will make me look dumb. How many things in my life have I not done out of the fear of looking stupid? *No mas.* I think that means "no

more." Not sure because I took French. *Je suis* Sammy and *Je suis* awkward.

Then there is the one reason I really want to write this book: I genuinely believe that our awkwardness and awkward moments are invitations to know more deeply the grace of God. Awkwardness is an invitation to vulnerability, and vulnerability is where intimacy and connection are found.

I want to be vulnerable. In my best moments, I believe in grace. My hope for this book is that its awkwardness will itself be an invitation to the kind of vulnerability that can only happen if grace is true.

Vulnerability is hard. But grace is true. So let's make some awkward.

Chapter One

DON'T WASTE YOUR AWKWARDNESS

2:08 p.m., Friday, July 18, at Drip Coffee

MAYBE IT'S BETTER TO START WITH AN OUTLINE? ALSO I find myself avoiding writing like an introvert trying to avoid a guy with an acoustic guitar at a party. I'm nervous about the topic. Is awkwardness relatable enough? Biblical enough? Sellable enough? Writing feels like trying to find the vein for a needle to release the blood that will save lives. Okay, that could be a seriously overinflated view of writing. I'm sitting in Drip. I just ordered a tasty tomato special. I took my first Uber today. I'm typing words because I need to get into a "flow," but it's not working. Also I saw *Dawn of the Planet of the Apes* with a friend while at "lunch." When I go to the movies during the day, I feel like Don Draper on *Mad Men*, except I'm not cheating on my wife and don't have a drinking problem. Oh, my sandwich

1

came so hold that thought. . . . That was delicious. I got it because I'm trying to lose weight. Getting fruit instead of chips feels like the adult thing to do, which is another way of saying the "unfun" thing to do. Being an adult is hard. Back to the book. Where should I start? This whole book feels like a giant beach ball greased up with sunscreen, and I can't quite hold on to it long enough to get under water without it slipping out of my hands again. Writer Anne Lamott says somewhere that most of the time you have to put butt in chair and write, write, write.[1] Seems like Super Glue would help. So it's 2:20 p.m. now, and I need some Super Glue.

If we had to make our relationship with awkwardness Facebook official, we probably would have to choose the "it's complicated" option. On the one hand, we are drawn to awkwardness. It's in the shows we love: *The Office, Arrested Development, Parks and Recreation, Modern Family,* and *New Girl.* It's in the actors and comics we love too: Seth Rogen, Jonah Hill, Zooey Deschanel, Amy Poehler, Ty Burrell, Ricky Gervais, Louis C. K., and Jim Gaffigan. We can't seem to get enough of awkwardness.[2]

And yet we are terrified of it, especially of being marked with what my friend Les Newsom calls the new scarlet letter: "A" for "awkwardness." One of our greatest fears is leaving a party only to have friends lock eyes with each other and complain about how awkward we are. We might be drawn to it, but there's still a social stigma in awkwardness we would like to avoid.

Maybe we haven't yet realized that we are both drawn to

awkwardness and afraid of it because deep down we are all awkward people. Just think about the last time you were in an elevator. Everyone's awkwardness shines a little brighter in an elevator.

I probably should define awkwardness. I don't mean wearing Crocs with socks (if you do, please gently lay down this book and text your most fashionable friend for help), or that you make small talk look harder than solving a Rubik's cube, or that you're the person everyone avoids introducing new people to at a party.

What I mean is that there's a gap between what you are and what you should be, a disconnect between the real you and the ideal you. What awkward moments (and people) do is simply shine the spotlight on that gap, revealing the cracks in our humanity, no matter how shiny and cool we may seem on the outside.

I remember the first time this came home to me in a real way, even if it's taken me years to learn how to articulate it. I was sitting in the world's saddest movie theater in Sumter, South Carolina, taking in *Meet the Parents* for the first time. And I suddenly realized that I was Ben Stiller. From the painful conversations to the desperate attempts at validation, I had never seen a movie that so perfectly captured the awkwardness that was my life.

Say the wrong thing. Do the wrong thing. Think the wrong thing. Repeat. Is that a life motto I can get tattooed somewhere?

For a long time I thought being awkward was a me-thing. But then I realized it's an us-thing. Some of us may feel more awkward than others, and some of us may act more awkward than others. At the end of the day, all of us not only have moments that make us feel awkward, we also have parts of our lives that are awkward to talk about.

One of my favorite awkward moments involves a friend. He was in college but home for the summer. The important thing to know is he was a full-grown man. And for some reason that day as he stepped out of the shower he decided that he would go downstairs wearing nothing but a towel and surprise his mom. And he did, by slipping off the towel and doing a naked dance as his mom talked on the phone.

The reason I love that story so much, besides how hilariously awkward it is, is that even though my friend was simply doing something he thought would be funny, the image illustrates a deep longing to be known and loved. The truth about awkward moments is that they're awkward because we long to be embraced as we are, not as we should be.

Again, that's what awkwardness is, the gap between what we should be and what we actually are. Life is awkward because it doesn't go the way that it *should* go. People are awkward because they don't do and say and think what they *should* do and say and think. All of us are awkward because all of us experience this gap in some way.

The gaps are hard to talk about, though, because they expose us for who we really are: someone who falls "short of the glory of God" (Rom. 3:23). The problem is, like the bad guys at the end of *Scooby-Doo*, we hate being exposed. But awkwardness is always an invitation to admit the truth about who we really are. And that makes us vulnerable, which is hard. Will anyone really love me if they see all the places where I fall short?

A few years ago I met with a student who had lived most of his life with a porn addiction. He got into it early by accident. But that accident gradually gave way to dependency, and what once seemed intriguingly gross transformed into a way of coping with the stresses and failures of life.

Over coffee he told me that sex, much less pornography addiction, was simply not something that was ever discussed in church. He grew up in one of those gospel-centered, published-author, preachers-whose-podcasts-you-download kind of churches. His family felt the same way. As in many good Southern families, sex was simply not something appropriate to talk about. Ever.

What he said nearly broke my heart: "Because no one ever talked about porn, I felt like it must be the worst sin in the world, and so I was so scared and ashamed to tell anyone about it." What my student was describing was shame.

One of the saddest realities of life is the things we need to talk about the most are the things we tend to talk about the least. Shame is often the culprit. Author and speaker Brené Brown says that shame only needs three things to survive: secrecy, silence, and judgment.[3] If you look behind your awkward moments, you will almost always find shame.

Shame is exactly what Adam and Eve experienced in the Bible in Genesis 3. After failing in a pretty spectacular way, they were incredibly afraid to meet God, so they covered themselves with fig leaves and hid. It was the first awkward moment in the history of the universe; it was the first walk of shame, too, and it happened to be away from God. It's hard to know exactly what Adam and Eve were thinking after they realized their sin. They seem to do a good bit of minimizing, blaming, and covering. Instead of going to God in their newly realized nakedness, they tried to handle it themselves. Why? Shame.

Shame, simply put, is the subjective experience of objective guilt. It's that moment where we know and feel that we've done something wrong. It's always easier to live in shame than in vulnerability, to try to hide and cover ourselves instead of going to God (and others) with our brokenness. Adam and Eve covered their nakedness and hid from God, rather than being vulnerable with him about what really happened. Shame is like the invisibility cloak in Harry Potter, except the reason you don't want people to see you is that you're afraid if they really did they would run.

A few months ago I was grabbing dinner with a friend, and we were talking about our weeks. That particular week had been hard for me because a pastor-friend in town had been invited to speak at the biggest ministry on our campus. So I started talking about how jealous I was of him, and how hard it was for me to be around him because I get really insecure over how gifted he is. As I was saying these things, I happened to glance behind me, and there sat his best friend. He'd heard everything but played it off really well. It's in the top ten awkward moments of my life, one of those moments when I wished I had Professor X's mutant powers so I could wipe away that memory from ever happening.

As I was driving home that night, though, it struck me that this awkward moment could actually be a gift of God's grace. A moment pregnant with awkwardness could also be a moment when friendship is born because the only thing worse than confessed insecurity and jealousy is unconfessed insecurity and jealousy, even if it does make things ten thousand times more awkward.

What God did for Adam and Eve in Genesis 3 is something we desperately need to look at. He looks for them, and instead of scolding them when he finds them, he asks them some heart-searching questions. When God asks questions he doesn't do so like a passive-aggressive mother-in-law, looking to scold or shame; he does so as a loving father who cares for the well-being of his children.

Then he does something so remarkable we could easily miss it. He tells them to take off the fig leaves because he has a new set of clothes for them to put on, clothes he himself provides from the skins of the newly named animals in the garden. Instead of shaming them, he covers their shame. Like a parent dressing a child, he clothes and protects them to keep them safe and warm. His gracious action is what enables them to risk vulnerability. Perhaps the apostle Paul had this in mind when he later wrote that "God's kindness is meant to lead you to repentance" (Rom. 2:4).

The story of Adam and Eve is the first place in the Bible that points toward salvation through sacrifice. In order for Adam and Eve to live, something had to die. In order for them to be covered, something had to be stripped. The Bible says this is exactly what Jesus came to do for us; the

Lamb of God was slain for the sins of the world. At the cross Jesus was stripped so that we might be covered. The reason we can be vulnerable is that the God of the universe was first vulnerable for us. Because he has secured our forgiveness—the once-and-for-all taking away of our shame—vulnerability goes from being a life-threatening act to a life-giving one.

When my youngest daughter was three, she played hide-and-seek badly. She would find her hiding spot, typically a closet upstairs, close herself in with the doors not quite shut, and then loudly begin to say, "In here! I'm in here!" until someone found her. She loved to hide, but she wanted to be found.

So do we. We love to hide from each other. We hide our flaws, our defects, and anything we feel will make us look like we don't have it all together. We hide how we're really doing, even from our closest friends and family. Because, like Adam and Eve, we're afraid the person who finds us will condemn and judge us. So we lock ourselves away, resolving to never share the things in our lives that are killing us: broken relationships with parents, lust that's blossoming into addiction, depression that's overwhelming us to the point of wanting to end it all, a relationship with food that makes us hate and do harmful things to our bodies.

But we still long to be found. It's why websites like PostSecret and Tumblr exist. They are places where we can talk freely about our struggles without running the risk of being judged by our family, friends, or potential employers. The problem with being vulnerable online with people who barely know us versus being vulnerable in real life with friends and family is that it never quenches the thirst we have to be both known and loved. Being found involves both: being really known and truly loved.

1:24 p.m., Saturday, July 19, in my bed

MIRACLE OF MIRACLES, THE KIDS SLEPT IN UNTIL almost eleven this morning. But then so did I. I stayed in bed until noon like I'm a college kid. My mom is visiting, which is why I had the luxury of sleeping in. Connecting with my mom isn't exactly easy. What do we talk about? Someone close to her is in jail right now, and it's affecting her way more than I thought it would. Sadly my first thought upon hearing the news was, *You should watch* Orange Is the New Black *on Netflix.* Maybe my spiritual gift is genuinely believing TV shows make everything magically better. Hard to describe the oneness I feel with Don Draper and Tony Soprano and Walter White and, oddly, Liz Lemon. Honestly, I probably watch television to fill the time normally spent being afraid to do something. Also started Stephen King's book on writing this afternoon. Even prayed that the Lord would make it helpful to me to start writing my book. That sentence still doesn't feel right. My book. Why should I write a book? Can I write a book? Those are the twin demons messing with me right now. "Can" and "should." Still no golden tablets from heaven telling me exactly what I should do.

When I say vulnerability, I don't mean the fake vulnerability that loves confession and hates repentance, the kind that we use as a tool to get others to like us. Vulnerability in the name of approval is at best a trick, at worst a way of deep deception. I mean the kind of vulnerability that brings the innermost thoughts out from behind the closed doors in our minds. The kind that begins to put words to our deepest struggles. It brings things from the secrecy of the dark to the transparency of the light.

This is where grace comes into the picture. We will never risk vulnerability unless we believe in the kind of grace that says you are loved where you are, not where you've been pretending to be.[4] The good news is that grace is precisely for those who've been hiding because they know they've fallen into that gap between what they should be and what they are. This is also the bad news about grace. It's only for those who have stopped pretending and admitted where they really are. It's for those who, like the tax collector in Jesus' parable in Luke 18, keenly feel the wideness of that gap between what they are and what they should be so they can only pray, "God be merciful to me a sinner."

The reason vulnerability is hard is that we don't believe in this kind of grace. Many of us aren't open about our struggles because grace hasn't moved from a concept to a reality.[5] We're like Isaiah in the temple: we'll never have a true sense of our brokenness until we meet the living God, and we'll never have a true sense of his grace until he meets us with his unspeakable forgiveness (Jer. 6). God's grace makes the vulnerability that used to seem impossible, possible. Because we know that his love and acceptance don't depend on what we do but on what he has done. So the moment we cry with Isaiah, "Woe is me," is the same moment we hear the voice of God singing over us, "I have loved you with an everlasting love" (Jer. 31:3).

It's the same with Adam and Eve: the moment they began to tell God what they had done was the same moment God began to cover their shame. This seems to be something like a principle in the Bible. The more you get to know God, the more you get to know yourself in all your awkwardness; and the more you get to know yourself, the more you get to know God in all his grace and mercy.[6]

Awkwardness is an invitation to vulnerability, and vulnerability is where intimacy and connection are born. Awkwardness is also an invitation to throw yourself upon the grace that makes vulnerability possible at all. In the words of author and speaker Adam Kotsko,

> Social orders arise and perhaps evolve and eventually fall, but awkwardness will endure as long as we remain human because it is what *makes* us human. What Ricky Gervais and Judd Apatow point toward . . . is indeed an awkwardness so awkward it becomes its own kind of grace—it is the peculiar kind of grace that allows us to break down and admit that we are finally nothing more or less than human beings who will always be stuck with each other and, more importantly, to admit that we are glad of it.[7]

At the end of the day, awkward people are the only kind of people God loves because awkward people are the only kind of people there are. I hope what follows in this book will be a kind of invitation for you—an invitation to embrace your awkwardness and be surprised that, as you do, you will find yourself becoming more intimate, more connected, and ultimately more human.

One of my favorite lines in movie history comes from a fortune-teller in Richard Linklater's *Before Sunrise.* Jesse (played by Ethan Hawke) and Celine (played by Julie Delpy) have met by chance on a train, and after an incredibly engaging conversation, they spend the night walking the streets of Vienna, where they run into a fortune-teller. They jokingly decide it would be fun to have her tell their fortunes. What she says is this: "Resign yourself to the awkwardness of life."

We could say resign yourself to your own awkwardness too. Resign yourself to the awkwardness of talking about where you are, not who you've been pretending to be. Resign yourself to the awkwardness of being vulnerable about your struggles with close friends and family. Resign yourself to the awkward reality that there will always be a gap between what you should be and what you are. Resign yourself to the awkwardness of God's work of grace in you to begin to close that gap while simultaneously making you able to talk about it. Resign yourself to the awkwardness of life.

Don't waste your awkwardness. It may be the very place you learn to be vulnerable and thus experience the grace of God.

Chapter Two

PARENTS ARE A GIFT
(You Can't Return Them)

10:57 a.m., Monday, July 28, at Drip Coffee

ENCOURAGING CONVERSATION WITH MY EDITOR LAST week. Write through the outline, he said. Sounds good, except that I have this constant buzzing in my head telling me that everything I do is inadequate. It's way easier not to start things than to start them. Also I'm incredibly distracted right now because there's a group text message going among my wife and good friends. We're watching the friends' dog, Rue, and she's refusing to come inside our house. She must sense that we're cat people. Or that we can barely take care of our kids, much less a dog. Almost every one of these sentences feels forced and terrible right now, like later Adam Sandler movies. How am I feeling about the book? Afraid to start. Afraid that I'm not a good writer. Worse, that I'm just an okay writer desperately trying to be good. I'm afraid of trying. Trying makes you suscep-tible to failure. And failure makes you susceptible to rejection. Better, then, not to try than to try and fail and look dumb and be pitied. Trying means trusting you can be enough to the people who need you. Two hipster girls were looking at me and smirk-ing as I walked into this coffee shop, and that's what I'm afraid of. Being smirked at. Do they know me? Do they know about @prodigalsam? Do they think I'm a plagiarist, a fraud, another religious hypocrite? Was I walking funny? Are my jeans too tight? My jeans are probably too tight. Are they smirking because I'm wearing tight jeans and a long sleeve shirt in ninety-five degree weather? Does my hair look stupid? I knew I shouldn't have put that Aveda clay in it and pushed it up a little. Stupid. Am I sweat-ing through my shirt? It's new and lightweight, which means you can see all the sweat that my more-hairy-than-I'd-like body is pumping out. Do they know me from somewhere? Did I take a class with them? Do they think I'm someone else? Their mildly depressed single friend from work? Okay. Time to write. Where do I start?

I don't mean to start this chapter off in a minor key and make you put this book down, depressed, and order a pizza. But the story I'm about to tell you in some ways is the story of my life. And it's a sad one, or at least this scene, this sea-son of my life, is a sad one.

On a spring day in 1993, my grandmother picked me up from school and dropped me at home, where things were off. A strange car was in the driveway. I heard a strange voice in the living room. Our priest sat on the edge of our couch. He had never visited our house before. I felt like a character in a mob film, slowly realizing that he's about to sleep with the fishes. (Fishes? Mobsters aren't English majors.)

This is how the conversation started. "Sammy, we need to talk to you about your dad." Now what you need to know is that by this point my dad had left home and was living in an apartment across town. And that's really all I knew. Well, that and that he had a new girlfriend, Amy, who was different from my mom. And way flirtier. I knew that too.

They told me more. My dad had been an alcoholic my entire life. He had also nursed a cocaine habit that had recently blossomed into a full-blown crack addiction. After an intervention by his sisters and some close friends, he had gone to a rehab facility in upstate South Carolina. My mind processed the words, but my heart held them at arms' length.

Devastated doesn't describe what I felt that day. It's hard enough when one of your parents leaves. It's way harder when he turns out to be a completely different person from who you thought he was. How can this person who wrestled with me in my bed, took me to football games, played count-less rounds of catch, taught me how to tie my shoes, took me to work with him, bought me coffee drowning in milk and sugar and a honeybun along the way, possibly be a drug addict? It's like finding out that Superman is Lex Luther.

What I remember most about that day was actually a different conversation. My dad called later that night and tried through tears to say that everything was going to be okay. We both choked up, the painful reality of this situation taking our emotional breath away, our literal breath too.

What a devastating realization it is that your parents are people—people who carry wounds and who create wounds too. Wounded people wound people,[1] whether they stay or leave. One of the keys to the wholeness we all long for is embracing the awkwardness of loving and forgiving our parents, wounds and all.

A counselor once told me that if I kept expecting my dad to be the kind of dad I wanted him to be, I would always be disappointed, but that if I could grieve the loss of that vision and pursue a friendship with him, we could be good friends. For some reason this was incredibly freeing to me. The counselor gave me the freedom to treat my dad like a normal human being.

Human beings are rarely everything we wish they would be. The inevitability of disappointment comes with relationship. And so we will be disappointed, especially by those human beings we're around the most, our parents.

This isn't an excuse for parents not to be the best parents they can possibly be to their children. There is no pass-go card like in Monopoly, letting parents happily skip over the day-in and day-out drudgery of life on Baltic Avenue. I'm learning that parenting is way more Baltic Avenue than Park Place.

Sometimes it takes becoming a parent to realize that your own parents are human beings. Frail. Fragile. Insecure. Wounded. The thing about being an adult is you're never quite sure you're doing the right thing. Multiply that by ten when you're a parent. You're trying your hardest not to screw up your kids all the while knowing the biggest reason your kids will be screwed up is you. That's why instead of a college fund for our children, my wife and I have a counseling fund.

In his book *How Children Raise Parents*, Dan Allender writes that all of us are born into this world asking two questions: "Am I loved?" and "Can I get my own way?"[2] It's the job of parents to answer both of these questions for us. How they do shapes us in powerful ways. The kind of parents you have depends on how they answered these two questions for you.

There are "Yes and Yes" parents. These are the parents who tried harder to be our friends than our parents. They told us they loved us. A lot. Maybe uncomfortably so. But they could never tell us no out of the fear of disappointing us and losing our love.

This is Amy Poehler's character in *Mean Girls*. Poehler plays Regina George's mom, and when Lindsey Lohan's character meets her for the first time, Poehler tells her, "There are no rules in this house. I'm not like a regular mom. I'm a cool mom." Then her daughter says, "Mom, please stop talking."

The sad reality of parents who only want to be our friends is that while we want them to engage us and meet us where we are, we also want them to love us enough to tell us no and stand up to us when we're wrong. We intuitively know that love doesn't always let us get our own way. Love loves enough to disappoint.

Then there are "No and No" parents. These are the parents we grew up resenting, trying to prove ourselves to. We were less their children and more their prisoners or their trophies. While they may have been proud of our accomplishments, it never felt like they were proud of *us*. They pressed "Start" on the performance treadmill of our lives, and we haven't been able to hop off ever since.

For some of us this included abuse. Emotional. Verbal. Physical. Sexual. It is possible for parents to forfeit the right of being parents through their own selfish, hurtful actions toward you. These parents also need our forgiveness, whether they know it or not. But forgiveness doesn't always mean restored relationship. The sad reality of life is that some relationships, even within the family of God, won't be restored until the new heavens and new earth. This both grieves us and frees us.

I recently had dinner with a friend who grew up with an abusive father. Her father never physically abused her, but there's a way, without ever raising your hand, of hitting your kids so hard they never recover. And he did, with moods and looks and words. One day her dad fell, hit his head, and slipped into a coma. She told me that as she held his hand in the hospital, the question that screamed in her mind was, *Why did you never hold my hand when I was afraid?*

It's hard to be warm toward a parent whom you've only ever known as cold and critical. I suppose the only thing that begins to till the iron ground of your heart toward a parent who has been hard on you is to remember that behind their arrogance and aloofness are hidden wounds and deep insecurities.

Then there are the "No and Yes" parents. No, you're not

loved, and yes, you can have your own way. These are the parents who are either workaholics or are so caught up in themselves that even if they don't leave, their presence is marked mainly by emotional absence. Parents who leave are by default "No and Yes" parents because their act of leaving answers both questions in a permanent way.

In a sense when a parent abandons you, it feels like them saying, "No, I don't love you enough to stay," as well as, "Yes, have your own way because I'm not here to tell you no." This is why divorce can have such a devastating effect on our ability to believe we can be deeply and truly loved.

In the movie *The Spectacular Now*, Miles Teller plays Sutter, a high-school senior trying to figure out life, relationships, his future, and himself. One of the missing pieces is a dad (played by Kyle Chandler) who left when he was young. Sutter decides to reconnect with his dad and finally tracks him down. They set up a visit, and Sutter is beaming with the possibility of a relationship. What happens instead crushes him. Instead of wanting to reconnect, resume the unspeakably weighty role of father in his now almost-adult son's life, Sutter's father is so consumed with drinking with the boys and chasing tail that he can't even stand to visit with his son for a night. The result on Sutter is devastating.[3]

The kind of parent all of us long for is the "Yes and No" parent. Yes, you are more loved than you could possibly know. And no, I love you too much to always let you have your way. I love you as you are, and my love is going to make you the best you that you could possibly be. To be clear, no parent can ever fully live up to this task. In the words of writer Michael Chabon, "A father is a man who fails every day."[4] The same goes for mothers.

This is the kind of father God is. He isn't naive to the sinfulness of his children. He hasn't closed his eyes to the choices we make that could only be described as selfish. He knows us truly, and yet he loves us deeply, not for anything that we have done, or could do. He doesn't love us because we're lovely. Rather his love makes us lovely.

And he isn't one bit afraid to tell us no. Someone once said that God always answers our prayers in one of three ways: yes, no, and wait. He tells us no not because he's oblivious to our needs or, worse, insensitive to them. He tells us no precisely because he knows our needs better than we know them ourselves. Scripture presents God as a father to trust and enjoy, not a boss to slave for and endure. This means sometimes he will overjoy us. And sometimes he will disappoint us. But he always does both as a good father who loves his children well and is not afraid to fight for them.

A few years ago my wife went of town for the weekend and left me to watch the kids by myself. At the time we had three, which is about three too many for a dad to watch for an entire weekend. When mom's away, dad will feed the kids like they're freshmen in college. We survived on pizza and fast food. And movies. Lots and lots of movies. If my wife keeps letting me watch the kids, they will see every single movie Netflix has to offer.

One of the movies we watched that weekend was *Finding Nemo*. I had seen it before, but my kids hadn't. Watching a movie with your kids changes the way you see it, because you start watching it through their eyes. At one point as we lay there, huddled in my bed, I started crying. Not full-on weeping, but fighting back tears, trying to push them back where they came from, but they wouldn't quite fit.

We got to the end of the movie when Nemo's dad is desperately doing everything he can to find and save his son, and a thought struck me: *I wish I had a dad like that.* A dad who spared no expense, faced every possible difficulty just to make sure I was safe and to hold me in his arms again.

And then another thought followed: *You do have a dad like that.* A heavenly Father who did far more than swim through the depths of the seas to find me. The words of Paul rang in my ears: "He who did not spare his own Son but gave him up for us all, how will he not also with him graciously give us all things?" (Rom. 8:32).

The key to loving your parents is knowing there is only one parent who perfectly says, "Yes, you are loved" and "No, you can't have your own way." His name is God. Every earthly parent will fall short, as hard as they might try, as good as they might be.

God says, "Yes, you are loved" like the best mothers. Some of the most neglected images in Scripture are the ones in which God himself compares his love for his children to that of a nursing mother and a mother hen. The eighteenth-century English pastor John Newton wrote, "The love, and tenderness . . . of ten thousand mothers . . . if compared with his, are less than a drop of water to the ocean."[5] God gives us an astounding image of the way he feels about us in the book of Zephaniah: a mother rocking her children, singing songs over them.

One of my most deeply spiritual experiences involved Dunkin' Donuts, the Dixie Chicks (I know), and the book of Galatians. I was sitting in Dunkin' Donuts, sipping coffee, reading the first part of Galatians 4, listening to music. My wife had recently made me download, against my carefully crafted and pretentious music taste, "Lullaby" by the Dixie Chicks. That song came on as I was reading Galatians 4:7, "So you are no longer a slave, but a son, and if a son, then an heir through God." Moments later the words from "Lullaby" rang not just in my ears, but in my soul, as a mother sings over her child, asking him how long he wants to be loved, promising him that she will never, ever let him go. The way a mother can't help but look at her newborn has nothing on the way God looks at his children. It was a powerful experience. (The donuts probably helped too.)

God also says, "No, you can't have your own way." His answer, like that of the best fathers, is never meant to crush the spirit of his child out of spite or jealousy, but instead to train and teach his child to be wise, to be patient, to persevere.

I've always loved the story of theologian J. I. Packer on his tenth birthday. He desperately wanted a bike. The trouble was just a couple of years earlier he had been hit by a bread truck and had badly injured his head. He had to wear a protective helmet from then on, no matter what he was doing. His parents knew that a bike would be both dangerous and foolish, so they gave him a typewriter, just what every ten-year-old boy longs for on his birthday. No doubt he was disappointed, but a beautiful thing happened. He began to write and kept writing. He has now written scores of books, and rumor has it he still uses a typewriter. Good parents love their children enough to disappoint them because they love them and deeply want what's best for them.

1:59 p.m., Wednesday, July 30, at Drip Coffee

SITTING DOWN TO WRITE AND I NEED TO CONFESS THAT I totally just avoided a guy I'm pretty sure I knew in college. I did the old "walk-by and pretend not to see him" move, later hoping he wouldn't hear the barista call out my name when my coffee was ready. Thankfully he was in the bathroom when my name was called. Why do I avoid people so much? Am I afraid of my painful inability to make small talk? If I could be given one superpower, I would ask for the ability to make small talk. Is it my embarrassment of feeling like a different person back in college? Sometimes I feel like I am one giant walking apology, constantly feeling sorry for things I haven't even done yet. Some people are walking exclamation points. I'm a walking semicolon. Cautious. Hesitant. Unsure. Also I'm drinking my coffee black right now like I've got something to prove.

The disappointing reality of your earthly parents is they will never perfectly love you this way. That means you're going to need a lot of forgiveness. And forgiveness is a long winding road. It's going to take the love of our heavenly Father to get us there.

My dad left home when I was twelve years old, and we have had an on-again, off-again relationship for the last twenty-two years, sometimes much more off than on. You never get over wanting a dad. Or maybe it's better to say you never get over wanting your dad to be a dad.

I remember vividly the conversation we had when I learned he was gone. This was after he had been placed in rehab for a crack cocaine problem. How a golden boy from a wealthy family in a small town in the middle of South Carolina develops a crack addiction is a long, complicated story with a familiar turning point: a father who was never able to tell his kids how much he loved them.

In some ways my dad and I are the same person. We both love food, music, basketball, and Clemson football; and we are both so sensitive we make a baby's bottom look hard. But more than that, my father never got the love he wanted from his dad. Therefore I never got the love I wanted from my dad. A father's rejection opens up a black hole of need that you try to fill by constantly seeking from everyone else the love and approval you never got from dad. This is my story. It is my father's too. No wonder we're so much alike.

When my dad moved out he got an apartment across town. This was before he was checked into rehab, but after he had starting smoking crack with his new girlfriend. She was the one who introduced him to it. The hard part was she seemed like a nice, pretty woman. But people are never what they seem. It's hard when you realize that about your parents.

That apartment was a dark place. Literally it was

dark—there was very little light from windows or lamps—but I mean more in the spiritual sense. There were stacks of *Penthouse* magazines everywhere, along with other objects whose function I didn't completely understand. In some ways it was a teenage boy's fantasy apartment, except for the fact that it belonged to the person who used to tuck me in at night.

My dad sat my sister and me down on the stairs of that apartment one night. He told us how our mom was saying that he was doing drugs and he wanted us to know it was not true. We were thirteen and nine at the time, and we loved our dad and wanted badly to believe him. So we did. My mom got all our anger. That's the worst thing about being the parent who stays in the picture: you get two anger-at-parents for the price of one.

I was angry, but I didn't realize it. All I wanted to do was sleep and listen to music and play video games. I had a Sega Genesis video game console, and I would take it on those supervised visits with my dad. It was the Sam to my Frodo. Always there for me, protecting me from bad things. Come to think of it, maybe that Sega was less like Sam and more like the ring.

My mom knew I was angry. She tried again and again to get me to go to counseling with her. I always dug in my heels. One time she came in my room and said, "That's it. You are going to see my counselor." I reached for the Easton baseball bat in my closet, held it up to her, and said, "I'm not going anywhere." She left the room in tears.

I read in *Wired for Intimacy* by William M. Struthers

that there's a big difference for a male child between the affirmation of your mom and the affirmation of your dad. Struthers wrote, "When a boy realizes he is other than his mother . . . who is it that tells him who he is, what he is to do, what he will become? His father. The father, the masculine voice, acts to inform, equip, instruct and model. In the absence of this voice, which at its best is loving, trustworthy and affirming, a boy is forced to look for whatever is available to discover who he is."[6]

When your mom affirms you, in some ways she's affirming part of herself, because you came from her. She carried you and pushed you out into this world. You are in a strange way an extension of her. With dads, it's different. When your dad affirms you, he's affirming what you have become. Your choices. Your achievements. You. Your mom might affirm who you are, but the affirmation of your dad approves of who you have become.

This, I think, explains why I'm so hesitant, why I'm so desperate for someone to tell me I'm doing a good job. That voice of affirmation has been missing my whole life. And when I'm being honest, I have to admit I don't know how to get that affirmation from my heavenly Father. I don't know how to get the voice that says, "This is my beloved Son, with whom I am well pleased" (Matt. 3:17).

Maybe this is why father-son bonding can feel so awkward. In most cases it's a man who was never affirmed by his father not knowing how to affirm a younger man who longs for affirmation. Maybe this is also why I hear the opening sounds of the show *Parenthood* and immediately burst into tears. What are parents? They are often people who never felt deeply loved or affirmed by their own parents.

In Michael Chabon's novel *Telegraph Avenue*, one of the main characters, Archy, about to be a father for the first time, has a sudden realization about what it means to be a dad:

> You never would get through to the end of being a father, no matter where you stored your mind or how many steps in the series you followed. Not even if you died. Alive or dead or a thousand miles distant, you were always going to be on the hook for work that was neither a procedure nor a series of steps but, rather, something that demanded your full, constant attention without necessarily calling on you to do, perform, or say anything at all. . . . an obligation that was more than your money, your body, or your time, a presence neither physical nor measurable by clocks: open-ended, eternal, and invisible, like the commitment of gravity to the stars.[7]

I could have never said it so eloquently or profoundly, but that's exactly the same awful thought I had on April 29, 2005, when I became a dad for the first time. My oldest daugther, Jayne McBride Rhodes ("Jayne Mac"), was born: sweet, calm, and bald. Very bald. We had to use a sticky substance just to get little bows to stay on her head.

I almost missed her grand entrance. My wife sent me to Walmart to pick up some DVDs to watch, *Newlyweds* with Jessica Simpson and Nick Lachey. There was a McDonald's inside that seduced me into a late-morning sausage biscuit.

By the time I got back to the hospital, things were moving quickly, and before I knew it I was staring into my daughter's struggling eyes, kissing the matted mess of hair on the top of her head, pretty sure I wasn't holding her the right way. The perfect metaphor of how it feels to be a father. Never quite sure you're doing it right. Almost positive you're not.

That's what it feels like to be a dad. To be keenly aware that you're not doing it right, not doing or being enough. My daughter is ten now, and it's harder to look her in the eyes, because those eyes saw her mom and me fighting just the other day. Her ears heard me saying things I later had to apologize for, first to her mom, then to her. To be a dad is to be someone who needs to be forgiven.

The greatest gift a dad—or any parent—could ever give his children is to never tire of saying, "I'm sorry" and "I was wrong" and "I love you." And to mean it. An imperfect father resting in the forgiveness of his perfect heavenly Father is free to be wrong, to apologize, to love from the heart with deep joy. In the words of professor and writer Jamie Smith, to be a dad is to be someone who promises to "love prodigals"[8] because he himself is one. Prodigal sons who've been welcomed home by their Father with kisses make the best dads.

A few years ago we were at a wedding in Augusta, Georgia. My daughter was six at the time, old enough to figure out that she loved to dance. As we walked through the doors of the reception, she made a beeline to the dance floor and was by far the first one out there. It's funny how different your children can be from you. My happy place at a wedding is in the corner with a plate full of food and a beverage in my hand. Hers is the dance floor.

As she was dancing, a few older girls showed up, and they really knew how to dance. And as they started breaking it down, I watched my daughter crumple on the dance floor, eyes burning like lasers through these girls. I could tell she was angry, jealous, and insecure. Later as we climbed into the minivan (I could write a whole other chapter on the shame of owning a minivan) to head home, she was still upset. I asked her what was wrong, doing that thing parents do when they try not to laugh and cry at the same time.

Through gritted teeth, she said, "Those girls. I hate those girls. They're better dancers than me." And my heart broke. Not because those girls could dance, but because I saw the same perfectionism I've lived with for almost thirty-five years worming its way into the heart of my six-year-old daughter. That perfectionism robs all joy because it fixates you so desperately on your own performance, with the promise that if you can just be perfect everything will be okay. What perfectionism doesn't tell you is that nothing will ever be perfect, you most of all.

Anne Lamott wrote, "Perfectionism is based on the obsessive belief that if you run carefully enough, hitting each stepping-stone just right, you won't have to die. The truth is that you will die anyway and that a lot of people who aren't even looking at their feet are going to do a whole lot better than you, and have a lot more fun while they're doing it."[9]

To be a dad is to be someone dedicated, not to being perfect, but to being there. No matter how often you stumble, to keep going, keep running, keep trying. Not someone who has it all together, but someone who walks together with you through it, mountains and valleys alike.

On a recent Father's Day I thought about the first time I ever held my now ten-year-old daughter, and I realized that it isn't *how* you hold her. It's *that* you hold her.

2:13 p.m., Friday, August 1, at Drip Coffee

WEARING A NEW SHIRT TODAY. IT'S GOT THOSE PERfectly lined creases down both sides of my rib cage that say, "Yeah, I haven't been washed yet. You got a problem with that?" I got it on sale from J. Crew. I love J. Crew, even though it feels like it went off to study abroad in Europe and has been a little pretentious ever since. I got my shirt on sale. Buying things on sale feels like winning something that still requires you to pay the other person. It's a lightweight shirt, which basically means it shows how much I sweat in any given situation throughout the day. Kind of like those old-school heat-sensitive Hypercolor shirts but for chronic over-sweaters. I used to sweat so badly in college that I bought that antiperspirant called Certain Dri that you would see in the deodorant section but always felt bad for it, like it had gotten lost in Walgreen's and the employees pitied it and put it on a shelf with its friends, but then those friends never ever talked to it. Certain Dri felt like superglue for your pits. Like your pits were dying from dehydration. You could hear your pits whispering, "Water . . ." if you listened closely enough. Okay, enough stalling. Back to parents.

We often hear that hope is borrowing from the past and the future to invest and infuse the present with redemptive meaning. That our stories can have happy endings no matter the broken beginnings. That our lives can know incredible change from the inside out. That generational sin can be broken. Lord, I believe. Help my unbelief.

From 1993 to 1998, all my visits with my dad were supervised. It was the court's way of saying, "We want you to see your kids, but we still don't trust you." This feels like most of the parent relationships I know: seeing you and trusting you are sometimes light-years apart. How can you trust someone who has broken your heart?

Not until I had kids of my own did I realize that's part of the deal. I'm going to break my kids' hearts in one way or another. They're going to need counseling, not because of life or their genes or their dating history, but because of me.

I once asked a wise older friend what being a godly parent looked like. His answer surprised me. He simply said, "Can you tell your kids that you were wrong and ask them to forgive you? If you can, then you're a great parent." Part of me hates this. Where are the effective discipline, the stirring family devotionals, the beatific family vacations?

Another part of me loves this. What my kids need most from me isn't my strategy but my sorry. I'm sorry for what I said. I'm sorry for what I did. I'm sorry for what they said. I'm sorry for what they did. I'm sorry that this life isn't what you thought it would be. I'm sorry that your mom and I couldn't give you what you needed. Or that we could but were too blind or selfish to see.

There is a story from the early church about a woman who went to be baptized and took her children with her with the simple prayer, "Be a God unto me and my children." Be what we need. Be what we know we should want. Be there for us when we want almost anything other than you. Be the only parent who can ever love us perfectly, faithfully, selflessly. Be the refuge of all parents struggling to make their way with their little bands in the wilderness. Be a God unto us. That's a prayer both parents and children alike can get behind.

When my first daughter was very little, sometimes when she cried she said, "Daddy my eyes are wet. My eyes are wet." She wanted me to take my hand and wipe away the tears from her eyes. As hard as I tried, I couldn't wipe away one tear before another one spilled down her cheek. It's a reminder to me that I can never possibly be the perfect father that she needs.

But there is a perfect Father to whom I can point her. And his love for his children never fails. One day he will wipe away her tears for good.

Not long ago I spent a week with my dad. We talked a lot about books, music, addiction, and our wounds. This was one of the favorite weeks of my life. God is making all things new, and I'm thankful to say one of those things is broken relationships between children and their parents.

Chapter Three

D *IS FOR DIVORCE*

10:13 a.m., Monday, August 4, at the
Women's Parlor at Rose Hill Pres.

I'M SITTING IN THE WOMEN'S PARLOR AT THE CHURCH
that gives me office space. *How did I get here?* I ask myself. The
answer is mostly because the Wi-Fi doesn't reach all the way to
the office I share with another person. I work best when alone
with the expectation that I won't be alone for long, so sharing
an office is actually not a bad gig, except when we're both
there at the same time. I'm learning that wanting to avoid writing is a normal thing. Yesterday was the anniversary of Southern
writer Flannery O'Connor's death, so I pored over her letters
looking for something quotable for Twitter. That was really my
motivation. Anyway, I found this: "Half of writing is overcom-
ing the aversion you feel when you sit down to do it."[1] Maybe
today I should outline this chapter. I've always been told I'm the

emotional woman in my marriage, so writing in the women's parlor feels scarily natural.

I don't remember many details about Thanksgiving Day my sixth-grade year. I'm sure we had a pig picking with my mom's family the Wednesday night before. That's always been our tradition. What do you do in our family before you get together and eat a big meal? Get together and eat a big meal. What I do remember about Thanksgiving is driving out to the country with my mom and sister to see my dad. He hadn't come home the night before, at least that's what I gathered when I got a little older. My dad was at work. He was a farmer, although if you met my dad, he wouldn't strike you as a farmer. A teacher or a writer or a musician maybe. But not a farmer.

We drove out into the field where he was, and my mom rolled down the window. She must have been angry. She knew he was having an affair, and not his first. My dad smelled like cotton fields and Marlboro Lights, two smells I still love and wish Urban Outfitters would combine and turn into a candle.

My parents fought that day. But then they had always fought. There was a hole in the wall behind my parent's bedroom door to prove it. Maybe the reason movies depict holes in walls as leading to magical places is because what really causes them is too painful to show. But as my dad snapped his head back when my mom tried to roll it up in the car window, I knew he probably wouldn't be home for dinner that night. What I didn't know was that he wouldn't be home for dinner ever again. Divorce might start with holes in the wall, but it always ends with holes in the hearts of the kids at home.

The Unexpected Legacy of Divorce, a book studying the long-term effects of divorce, closes with a toast given by a child of divorce at his friends' wedding:

> To many here today it feels strange to find that one of us is getting married. It's strange because we are a generation of cynical children when it comes to marriage. We came of age during a time when divorce became an acceptable alternative . . . the effect on us is one of caution, of skepticism. Who needs marriage? It's an outdated institution. Why be burdened? But while we were uttering these cynicisms, we were privately nurturing the hope that we could rediscover and experience that romantic and very profound magic that we had heard existed in a far-off time—to see marriage through innocent eyes.[2]

That toast goes straight to the heart of what most children of divorce believe about love. On the one hand, we are deeply skeptical of the possibility of lasting love. On the other hand, we long for it. Love is like a unicorn to the children of divorce (don't worry, this isn't the only unicorn reference in this book!). You badly want it to be real, but you are nearly positive it's purely mythical.

This is the legacy of divorce: children who are simultaneously skeptics *and* romantics when it comes to love. Watching your parents' marriage crumble makes you long for a spouse who will never leave you, while at the same time being almost sure they will.

They say that cigarettes are the silent killer. (It's like they forgot about cats.) But I think divorce is far more silent and deadly than cigarettes. One slowly kills the body. But the other slowly kills love. As novelist Margaret Atwood noted: "A divorce is like an amputation; you survive, but there's less of you."[3]

One sunny day in the spring of 1993 my dad, sister, and I unlocked the front door of my dad's apartment to find my mom trying to break in through the sliding glass doors in the back. She knew that my dad and his girlfriend were smoking crack, but she needed evidence. She couldn't afford a private detective, so she hired herself for the job.

Finding your mom breaking into your dad's apartment to collect evidence that she could use against him in court may, in fact, be the perfect image for divorce. No one goes to the altar envisioning this moment, even if the way your about-to-be husband proposed was tipsily at a horse race. The odds might be stacked against you, but ending up breaking and entering means the odds were avalanched against you, and you had no idea.

If you don't happen to come from a broken home, here are four things you need to know about what it's like when your parents get divorced.

1. *Watching what's supposed to be the most stable relationship in your life crumble before your very eyes makes you slightly suspicious of relationships.* Did I say slightly? I

meant incredibly. It means when you sing along with friends to The Darkness's "I Believe in a Thing Called Love," you sing it less like a declaration and more like a question. Do I believe in a thing called love? Because the rhythm of my dad's heart seemed to lead him into the arms of not my mom.

Tim Keller, a pastor and author in New York, was asked during a Q&A on Twitter what makes someone a good parent. What he said surprised me. He said someone once told him that the best way to be a good dad to his kids was to be a good husband to their mom. This seems a little counterintuitive until you realize that what your kids need most from their dad is a model of what real love looks like in the flesh. The best person to show them that is a dad who loves his wife. Divorce makes real love seem impossible. And in the worst cases, it makes you think you're not worthy of it.

2. *Divorce makes you feel compelled to fix your parents.* And trying to fix your parents is a supremely terrible way to spend your life. In my case I tried to become a spiritual mentor to my dad and a surrogate husband to my mom. Basically just your average thirteen-year-old kid. Riding my bike, playing baseball with my friends, possessing the same authority in our home as a forty-year-old man. Normal kid stuff.

In my sister's case it meant a severe case of obsessive-compulsive disorder that included both obsessive hand washing and compulsive shopping for school supplies. Life feels so out of control you grab at anything that gives you the illusion of order, so you find things to prop up your life. You become like Jonathan Silverman and Andrew McCarthy in the movie *Weekend at Bernie's*. Your life is over, dead. So you need anything and everything to prop it up, take it to parties, make it feel alive. The out-of-control feeling begins as you slowly realize you can no more fix your parents' marriage than you can marry your parents.

3. *Divorce makes you feel not so much like it's your fault but like you're faulty.* I remember counselors wanting to make sure my sister and I knew that my parents' divorce wasn't our fault. I can't speak for everyone from a broken home, but I never felt like it was my fault. My parents didn't get married because of me. They didn't get divorced because of me either. Their divorce wasn't my fault. But it did make me feel faulty, like something was deeply wrong with me.

One of my friends describes his parents' divorce by saying his dad filled the house with gas and then his mom lit the match. Kids of divorce didn't start the fire, but we are burn victims. Parts of ourselves, our lives, will never be the same again, never look the same. We didn't start the fire, but we will carry the marks of our parents' divorce forever. And if you've made it through the last couple of sentences without thinking about Billy Joel's best/worst song of all time, "We Didn't Start the Fire," I'm impressed.

4. *Two Christmases aren't as great as they sound.* Make that three if you then get married. Or maybe four if your

spouse has divorced parents. I think four Christmases is the maximum possible unless your family is really into polygamy and there were multiple divorces, in which case I'm so, so sorry. Because three Christmases have been enough to do us in. Who doesn't want a triple amount of last-minute gifts wrapped in guilt and shame?

Divorce has a way of making you choose a parent, or at least feel like you have to. Who will you live with? Who will you celebrate holidays with? Who will get more time with the grandkids? Sometimes the choice will be easy. In my case my dad was the one who left, and it took a long time and a lot of counseling to realize that his leaving meant I could decide whether I still wanted a relationship with him. And I do. But even as our relationship has gradually improved over the years, there aren't enough Christmases to make our time together feel full. It's like we're constantly playing catch-up, getting to know each other, over and over and over. Divorce has a way of estranging you from your parents, if not by the emotional damage, then purely by the limits of time and space.

We own a house in Statesboro, Georgia. If you had walked up to the house three years ago, one of the things you would have noticed immediately was lush, green ivy crawling up the right side of the house, just underneath a big bay window. The ivy took years and years to grow. We planted it not because we love ivy or have green thumbs. We planted it to cover a crack in the foundation.

Then a sad thing happened to our beautiful ivy. We hired a yard guy to cut our grass, and without asking, assuming we wanted him to clean up the beds around the house, he ripped out all the ivy. What was once a barely visible fracture had grown into an eight-inch gap in the foundation of our house.

Divorce is like a crack in the foundation of the lives of the children who live through it. It's easy to cover it over as though nothing happened. It's hard to deal with its effects on our lives, seen and unseen.

By the way, the crack in our house is still there. We haven't dealt with it yet. Raise a glass to avoiding your problems.

12:43 p.m., Friday, August 7, at Drip Coffee

ELVIS IS PLAYING IN MY COFFEE SHOP RIGHT NOW. I'VE never gotten Elvis. He's always seemed like a cliché to me. I think if he had been alive in the late 1990s, he would've been an Abercrombie model rather than a singer. I do appreciate his love for food though. The man could eat. Any man who reportedly dies eating peanut butter, bacon, and banana wrapped in white bread while sitting on a toilet is okay in my book. Every foodie's dream is to die doing what they love: eating. Maybe my problem is that Elvis could dance. I'm always a little suspicious of a man who can dance, which feels like a dog who can talk.

God hates divorce. That's what the prophet Malachi wrote. I hate divorce too. Not because I'm incapable of it. Or because I hate my parents. Or because I don't think there aren't justifications for divorce. Adultery and abuse come to mind.

I actually think my parents should have gotten a divorce. It's hard for me to write that because I wish they hadn't. But vows had been so deeply broken I'm not sure they could have been repaired this side of the new heavens and new earth. I believe God can redeem seemingly unredeemable marriages, make broken ones whole. I also believe sometimes he doesn't. Sometimes his grace lets us learn from consequences and make new decisions. If I've learned anything from my parents' divorce, it's that marriage is hard. It's also worth fighting for. That's the tension, isn't it?

Teddy Roosevelt wrote:

> It is not the critic who counts; not the man who points out how the strong man stumbles, or where the doer of deeds could have done them better. The credit belongs to the man who is actually in the arena, whose face is marred by dust and sweat and blood; who strives valiantly; who errs, who comes short again and again, because there is no effort without error and shortcoming; but who does actually strive to do the deeds; who knows great enthusiasms, the great devotions; who spends himself in a worthy cause; who at the best knows in the end the triumph of high achievement, and who at the worst, if he fails, at least fails while daring greatly, so that his place shall never be with those cold and timid souls who neither know victory nor defeat.[4]

It's funny how we so often apply this generally to life, but not specifically to marriage. To be married is to have your face "marred by dust and sweat and blood." At the wedding reception, when the bride and groom go to cut the cake, right before they smear it into each other's faces, the caterers should bring out a bowl full of dust, sweat, and blood instead. Then maybe the couple should have a quick conflict resolution session with the pastor who married them. I don't know. I'm still working out the kinks on my idea for a realistic wedding reception.

One of the perks (or curses) of my job is marrying students. (That last sentence is a case study in the importance of context.) One couple I married asked if they could write their own vows. Normally I say a flat no. I'm a fan of traditional words that have been used for years that somehow bind us and our marriages together. But this time I hesitantly agreed. One of the lines they both worked into their vows was this: "I promise not to divorce you." I realize it's the same sentiment as "Till death do us part," but this formulation really stood out to me.

Part of me resisted the line. It feels a little arrogant and naive to pretend to know how our lives will go. What if he turns out to be an alcoholic whose temper spills out in abusive ways in the home? What if she meets Mr. Right 2.0 and has a secret fling for three years? Can you really in good conscience promise not to divorce someone without being able to know the future?

Another part of me admired their commitment to each other. Even if he becomes an alcoholic abuser, or she, a restless housewife, the promise to forgive in a way that moves toward reconciliation, however difficult, is beautiful. I think the best metaphor we have for the kind of love God has for us is that he is a God who marries us with eyes wide open and promises to never divorce us regardless of how unfaithful we turn out to be.

When God says he hates divorce, he doesn't mean he hates the divorced. He means that the kind of love he has for his people is best captured by a one-sided marriage that he promises will never end in divorce. That's the kind of love he's come to create in his people. For him. For the church. And for husbands and wives.

God's love is the only love that can sustain a marriage because it is the only love that can promise it's never going anywhere. Our love is too frail, too fragile, to possibly sustain our marriages. German Lutheran pastor Dietrich Bonhoeffer said that it is not our love that sustains our marriages; our marriage becomes the place to sustain our love.[5] The only way to "divorce-proof" your marriage is for God's love to sustain your marriage so that, in turn, your marriage can sustain your love.

Divorce warps our understanding of love. It makes us simultaneously romantic and cynical about it. I'm reminded of this every time I watch *The Bachelor*. On the one hand it is about the quest to find the soul mate you've been looking for your entire life. On the other hand it is a game show where the goal is not to be eliminated, to get the rose at all costs. Get the rose, and you stay in the hunt for love. If you don't get the rose, the show's producers should at least be generous enough to give you a cat.

The Bachelor, in a pretty incredible way, shows how

really disillusioned we are with love. We over-romanticize what love can do for us instead of being realistic about what it demands from us. And we are cynical enough to reduce it to a game to entertain the masses. It's *The Hunger Games* but with roses, group dates, and show host Chris Harrison.

The only thing that can mend the hearts of those of us coming from broken homes is a love deeper than romance that melts our cynicism. A love that is subversive in its power. A love that stares into the abyss of our souls and says with compassionate conviction, "I'm not going anywhere." A love that knows us at our worst yet moves toward us still.

When the apostle John wrote about Jesus, he said that knowing him was like being able to see, to touch, to hear love in the flesh, that if he had written down all the unbelievably loving things Jesus did, there wouldn't be enough libraries in the world to hold all the books he could have written. Why? Because Jesus was so perfectly and purely full of love that every waking moment of his life, love flowed from him into the lives of others in ways that left them different from how they were before. John wrote that it wasn't that we first loved him, but that he first loved us.

It was and is a love free of sentiment, yet full of compassion. A love that led Jesus to do hard things, the hardest of which was setting his face and picking up a cross to die the kind of death only the most unloving deserve to die. Has the world ever known a man so free of self-love that he would be willing to embrace a death he didn't deserve so that those he loved might live a life they also don't deserve?

The strength to fight for love is only found in a love so strong it fought for us. The love of the cross that says nothing you've done is beyond forgiveness, nothing you've messed up is beyond repair.

Chapter Four

THE PORN IN MY SIDE

3:30 p.m., Wednesday, October 1, at Drip Coffee

I HAVEN'T WRITTEN ANYTHING IN ALMOST TWO MONTHS. That's next-level procrastination. I nearly pitched it all and started over until a friend convinced me not to. Good friends stop you from doing stupid things, or they at least try to. Also maybe they lie a little about your work being better than it probably is. At least that's the kind of friends I want. Friends who believe in you but don't buy your crazy. My sister recently asked how the book was going, and I said it really wasn't, and she said maybe you're "awfulizing" a little. Suddenly I had a word that made sense of my entire life. *Awfulizing.* Quit trying to tell me it's not a word, spell check, because it's kind of my signature move. Making people think you're perpetually on the verge of disaster/ hurting yourself even though life is totally normal and pretty okay. Right here! I think I found the title for my autobiography:

The Awfulizer. Sounds like a sad superhero, but I have to admit my ability to make any situation sound worse than it is in reality is a special power I possess.

I've never been dumpster diving for food or furniture. But I have been dumpster diving for porn. Maybe I should explain. I was sixteen, and my friends and I were at an abandoned high school playing hacky sack. That's right. Hacky sack. It's perhaps better known as tiny soccer for stoners. I'm not sure which I'm less proud of, climbing into a dumpster to fish out a couple of dirty magazines or admitting I've played hacky sack.

As we were playing, an older friend from youth group pulled up in his truck and started throwing bags of trash into a dumpster. Naturally we went over to say hello. Almost as soon as we did, he said, "You guys don't need to come any closer. I'm throwing away some magazines y'all don't need to see." Immediately I felt like Adam and Eve as the serpent whispered to them in the garden. I wanted whatever was in that dumpster. Bad.

So as the sun set, we all drove away. Fifteen minutes later I was back and climbing into the dumpster to pick my forbidden fruit.

In some ways when I think about my history with lust in general, and pornography in particular, this is the image that makes sense of it and is very, very sad. Lust has a way of killing love so that it reduces you to looking for it in a dumpster. Lust takes you to places you never imagined you would go. And when it does, it only increases the belief that if anyone really knew where lust had taken you, they could never possibly love you.

I'm getting ahead of myself. Let me take you back to the beginning where I fell in love with lust.

When Dad left home he also left behind a stack of dirty magazines that thirteen-year-old me found. A teenage boy going through adolescence is like Indiana Jones. He's looking for the Holy Grail, and that holy grail is pictures of naked people. His dedication to finding it knows no bounds. That was me the summer of 1992. I found my holy grail in the top drawer of an old cabinet in the garage.

I quickly found that lust could fill the holes of love left by my parents' ugly divorce and my dad's absence, at least for a little while. Then my leaky heart would deflate again, like a float with an invisible puncture, and I would fill it up with lust again, just long enough to feel full before the inevitable feeling of emptiness set in again. Habits developed, rituals set in, ones that take years to form and years to undo.

The lie of lust is twofold: one, that it will satisfy you, and two, that you are alone in struggling with it. You learn pretty quickly, however, that its satisfaction is fleeting and that those living under its power are many. But we still struggle not to believe the fictions lust tells us. Old lies die hard.

My problem with lust started at thirteen, and it is by no means finished with me yet. It has taken many forms. It started with magazines. Then straining through scrambled adult channels, rushing to catch the three minutes of free previews on pay-per-view. Computers made it easy;

smartphones, even easier. If you love anything enough, you'll make time for it. I've made a lot of time for lust.

The trick of lust is that it is the counterfeit of love. It looks good, feels good, and best of all it doesn't cost you anything. Real love demands sacrifice, but lust does not, unless you consider the sacrifice of ever knowing real love. Then lust costs you far more in the end.

Over and over again in my life, I've resolved to stop lusting. Time and time again, like Jake Gyllenhaal in *Brokeback Mountain*, I come back to my Heath Ledger and say, "I just can't quit you. I wish I knew how to quit you."

One of those times was the summer after college. Someone had given me a copy of *Every Man's Battle*. If you haven't read it, imagine a football coach yelling at you in book form to go out there and tackle lust. And, man, did I try. Hard. No porn. No masturbation. No crossing lines with your girlfriend. No lingering, roaming, glazed eyes. Let's tackle lust.

That same summer the craziest thing happened. I was browsing books with my girlfriend (now wife) at Barnes & Noble and must have browsed a little too long because I needed to make a visit to the men's room. I was fighting the good fight, avoiding the top row of the men's rack like the plague. I walked into the bathroom, opened the stall, and lying on top of the changing table were several dirty magazines practically calling out to me, "Come on over, big boy." I ran out of that bathroom. Okay, I walked really fast out of that bathroom. This was my Manassas, one of the few battles I ever won in the Civil War of Lust that rages in my soul.

Every Man's Battle ended up being just one more book I read in my resolve to stop lusting. The old habits and rituals came back. C. S. Lewis wrote, "Only those who've tried really hard to be good know how bad they really are."[1] That was true with lust for me. My counselor said the way you know you're addicted to something is you can stop but you can't stay stopped. That was also true.

Part of the struggle of lust is the guilt and shame it leaves behind in its wake. Lust is a bad strategy to deal with guilt and shame because it always leads to more guilt and more shame. But for many of us, it's the only way we know how to ease the burden of the guilt and shame we've been carrying for years.

In the movie *Her*, Joaquin Phoenix plays a man who falls in love with an operating system because he's terrified of real intimacy. Samantha, the operating system, is the perfect partner because her entire existence revolves around meeting his needs. There's a scene in the movie where he and Samantha spend a weekend in the mountains together, him in a cabin with her by his side through his phone. They sing a song together called "The Moon Song" in which the songwriter confesses he feels safe in the relationship precisely *because* they're at a safe distance from each other. False intimacy is attractive because it keeps us "safe" by distancing us from real intimacy, which always carries the risk of being hurt.

One of the things that makes lust so attractive to us is that intimacy is hard. All of us have a deep desire to be fully known and truly loved, yet at the same time we're terrified at the possibility. Who would love us if they fully knew us? Lust offers us an alternative—to be "loved" without being known and to "know" without having to love.

Like any cheap alternative, lust works fantastically for a little while, then it begins to break down like the fake Rolex I bought on Canal Street in New York. It looked real and felt real. And it made me feel good until the day it stopped ticking and came apart. Lust has the same effect in our lives.

Often lust is just a bad strategy for dealing with shame. For many of us, the shame we carry was born in sexual sin. Some of us carry the shame of being sexually used. We live in denial that what happened to us was really abuse. But denial can never cover over the marks of shame left on our souls.

When I was thirteen years old, a neighborhood friend took advantage of me. He was sexually experienced. I was sexually naive, not knowing anything about sex in general, much less sex with self. He was eager to teach me. Two separate times he did. The second one was over Labor Day weekend at a family friend's lake house. Looking back, I understand now what I didn't understand then. Abuse doesn't always make itself loudly known. More often it is carried out in the quiet manipulation of trust and friendship.

I remember sitting in pre-algebra class the next day being sure that even though he went to a different school, he had told everyone I knew what had happened. I was still trying to process it myself. Was I gay? Up until that point I had only ever liked girls and was still pretty sure I did. Then how do you explain what happened that weekend? The one thing I was sure of was that I couldn't tell a soul. And I didn't, for nearly ten years, until I finally told my now wife one night in the car in the drive-thru at Wendy's. (I would like to take a moment to thank Wendy's, specifically their spicy chicken combo and chocolate Frosties, for getting me through some hard times. Wendy's: bad for the body but so, so good for the soul.)

In his book *The Wounded Heart*, Dan Allender says that after experiencing abuse on any level, your relationship with sexuality becomes confused.[2] In some of us it kills the desire for sex. In others abuse awakens it, like a Frankenstein of sexual desires coming to life for the first time. And it is scary how much you can't control it, no matter how much you might try. The latter was the case for me. My relationship with masturbation became obsessive, compulsive even.

Sex with yourself is the saddest sex there is. Not because sexual desire is unhealthy. It's not. Sexual desire is one of the most precious gifts God has given us. New little people are formed because of it. Relationships are filled with joy. And an entire book of the Bible, Song of Solomon, is devoted to the pleasure it brings.

But when our desire for sex begins to push past the bounds of our desire for relationship and intimacy with God and with others, then sex itself becomes a kind of God we worship. In "Take Me to Church," singer-songwriter Hozier describes how sex can replace God. The problem is, as C. S. Lewis wrote, anytime you turn a gift of God *into* God, the gift immediately becomes a demon.[3]

8:45 a.m., Friday, October 3, at Drip Coffee

I GOT A BANANA FOR BREAKFAST BECAUSE I'M TRYING to watch my weight. Weight has always been a source of shame for me and now I feel shame that my shame has affected my kids. If you saw my kids you would think they look like normal, healthy kids. Why do I look at them and feel the overwhelming urge to comment about their weight? Just last week I told my son twice—twice!—that if he ate any more, his clothes wouldn't fit. Somehow I see my kids as a reflection of my own failure. The struggle of parenting is to stop seeing your kids as a reflection of you and start seeing them as a reflection of the image of God, full of inherent beauty and wonder. The goal can't be skinny. It has to be healthy. Not self-loathing, but self-control. A half-eaten banana sits looking at me from beside the laptop on the table as I write this. Peeling a banana is like getting undressed for the doctor. You know what's about to happen will be good for you, but you're not going to like it. Right. Time to put on the *Guardians of the Galaxy* soundtrack and write a little around lust. . . .

Several years into ministry I ended up in a six-month recovery program for sex addicts. I had been in counseling for a few years before it became clear that maybe something a little more intensive would be good for me. The counseling I had done up to that point was helpful, but the deep change I desperately needed wasn't happening, at least not as fast as I wanted. Counseling, or therapy as it's known to normal people (i.e., not Christians), has become something that's done less as a way to deal with traumatic events and more as a way of life. Like a good pair of jeans, a good counselor should fit and not make you hate yourself more. And just as it takes time to break in a new pair of jeans, it takes time for a counselor to break you down.

If you haven't spent one night in a quiet room with two professional counselors, eight sex (or "lust," for the more squeamish) addicts, and a bowl full of Wint O Green Life Savers the addicts nervously, obsessively crush like Tic Tacs, then you haven't truly lived. It's like sending yourself to middle school detention. Or better yet, it's like *The Breakfast Club*, minus the cool soundtrack. It's both depressing and incredibly life giving. A friend likes to say the two most life-giving words in the English language are *me too*. This was that times ten. Well, times eight, for my math majors.

The problem for most of us who end up in recovery is that we can't stand living in reality, so we don't. And the more we don't, the more life around us begins to fall apart. Relationships. Jobs. Finances. The more they begin to crumble, the more reality becomes a place to escape from, not live in. Lust is typically a strategy for dealing with the disappointment and difficulty of reality. In his article about drug addiction, English comedian and actor Russell Brand put it well: "Drugs and alcohol are not my problem, reality is my problem, drugs and alcohol are my solution."[4] Substitute "drugs and alcohol" with "lust," and I could have written that sentence.

If you had told know-it-all-seminary me who had answers for everything, including the kinds of counseling that were and were not biblically approved, that now-me has learned (and grown) so much from a twelve-step-based recovery group, I would have punched you in the face with one hand as I gave you a biblical counseling book with the other. The bad news about our stories is we don't have control over the arc. The good news is that God does, and he takes us to some wonderfully surprising and healing places. In the words of philosopher Dallas Willard, "Anyone who thinks God only blesses what is 'right' has had a very narrow experience and probably does not really understand what God has done for them."[5]

Throughout my time in that recovery group, the story of Naaman from 2 Kings 5 was much on my mind. Naaman, a powerful commander of the king's army in Syria, contracts leprosy and is desperate for a cure. The Israeli slave girl in his house tells him he should go see Elisha, the powerful prophet of her God Yahweh. So he loads up his entourage, packs up an obscene amount of silver and gold (three million dollars, at least by the most conservative estimates), and heads straight to the palace of the king of Israel to pay for his healing.

The king of Israel angrily turns him away. Elisha hears word of it and tells the king to send Naaman his way. So Naaman and his entourage show up at Elisha's house and stand triumphant at his door. But instead of coming out himself, Elisha sends a messenger, who tells Naaman to go wash in the Jordan River seven times.

This may sound easy and great, but the problem was at least twofold in Naaman's mind (three if you count that this message came through a lowly servant). Number one, Elisha isn't offering a cure but a ritual cleansing that anyone could do. That was an offense to Naaman's sense of self-importance. To be cured is to be set apart, to be special. To be clean is—well, anyone can be clean. And the difference between cured and clean isn't a small one.

Number two, the Jordan River is neither the biggest nor most beautiful river in the world. It feels more like a lake to boat in rather than a river to swim in. Plus Naaman had his own beautiful rivers at home, like the Damascus River, that he could enter to be made ritually clean. There was nothing special about the Jordan River.

This was Naaman's problem. He thought he was more special, more important than other people. The Bible calls this pride. If fear of intimacy is often what leads us into the embrace of sexual sin, pride is what often keeps us there. Pride says no one can ever know about this. Pride says I can handle this on my own. Pride justifies destructive behavior in the name of the self-comfort that seems terrifying to live without.

Sitting in that awkwardly lit counseling room on Thursday nights for half a year, I felt like Naaman, reeling from the humility of being there, telling myself I wasn't like these other people. What I've learned (the hard way) is that I'm just like them, and they're just like everyone else. Even if some form of sexual addiction isn't your thing, something else is, statistically speaking. Addiction doesn't distinguish when it comes to hurting people trying to escape the painful reality that is life.

And the power of addiction is real, whether it's a word that's part of your vocabulary or not. Few writers have had better insight into addiction than David Foster Wallace. In his masterpiece *Infinite Jest*, he describes the way Joelle van Dyne, a character deeply addicted to free-base cocaine and who oddly wears a veil every day, feels when she's high. "The 'base frees and condenses, compresses the whole experience to the implosion of one terrible shattering spike in the graph, an afflated orgasm of the heart that makes her feel, truly, *attractive*, sheltered by limits, deveiled and loved, observed and alone and sufficient and female, full, as if watched for an instant by God."[6]

A twelve-step recovery group became my Jordan River. I'm sure there will be others. But washing there has taught me a few things, like you won't be cured but you can be clean. That's actually a decent definition of what theologians call sanctification. There's no such thing as being cured of sin in Christian life, but repentance and real, progressive change is possible. This doesn't happen in a vacuum. That's the other thing I've learned. Change happens in a community of people who are being brutally honest about what's going on inside their hearts and heads. This should be the church. Most often, it exists in small pockets and certain fringes around the church. This isn't the church's fault. It's ours. The Bible loves honesty. Jesus does too. It's we who don't.

I meant to say at the beginning of this section that if you are a conservative, Reformed, gospel-centered, Bible-believing, evangelical Christian, I want you to put down the book for a minute, slide into your Chaco sandals, and go for a quick walk while I talk about a few things that could be uncomfortable. But they need saying. We want life to be like our theology—neat and tidy, well reasoned, and well explained. The trouble is life isn't always like that, thank God, because if it were, we would read about God but not actually need him to be present in our lives with power to save and heal in ways for which we don't have categories. As Martin Luther reportedly said, "Bad theology is a cruel taskmaster."[7] Amen. We could add, "And good theology is a poor savior."

Recently I met with a student over coffee. I was nervous because I knew that the conversation we needed to have was not the one we typically had. I needed to tell her that I thought she might be a sex addict, someone using sex to deal with life. So with much prayer and awkward hesitation, I did. As we talked, something beautiful happened: her shame began melting away. For years she had been scared to tell anyone about what was happening, about the addiction that was forming, because the impression given from parents and church was that this sin was so extra-sinful it was like Voldemort. You dared not mention its name in public, unless you wanted to be leered at and shushed into a corner. Guys could struggle with lust but not girls. That was what shame was telling her.

The desire to act on lust is fueled by the shame of not being able to stop acting on it. And the shame of acting on it is dealt with by doing it again. And again. And again. It's a cycle only the gospel can fully break. The gospel that says, "I see your shame, and I still love you, and the way you can know I love you is that I've done something about it."

In Hebrews we learn that Jesus went to the cross

"despising the shame." It would be better to say he knew how covered in shame he would be but considered it a small thing compared to what was on the other side, a restored relationship with people like you and me, people whose shame has taken us to the country of addiction and whose addiction keeps us living in the land of shame.

The good news is that Jesus doesn't shame us out of our sins. He loves us out of our sins.[8] Since love can break the power of shame, it can also break the power of lust. The only place we can be truly unveiled and loved isn't in an act that makes us feel that way for a moment, but at a cross that says we are loved whether we feel it or not. A cross that says, "I'm here because I know all that you've ever done. And I'm here because I love you more than you'll ever know."

This idea that instead of shaming us out of our lust Jesus loves us out of our lust really began to come home the more I read John 4. Jesus has a conversation with a woman so eaten up with sexual shame that he finds her drawing water in the hottest part of the day in order to avoid the judgment she feels from the other women in her town. She's known to us simply as the Samaritan woman. (Every time I read that phrase I hear Guess Who's "American Woman": "Sa-mar-i-tan wo-man, get away from me-ee!")

Over the course of the conversation between Jesus and the woman, we learn a few things about her. She's been through more marriages than Katy Perry has outfit changes in a concert. The man she's currently living with isn't her husband. It's reasonable to think she not only has been used by men but also has used them for her own purposes, and that sex probably was at least partly one of the purposes. Words like *abuse* and *addiction* might be ones she would use if she were alive in the twenty-first century and telling her story.

There seem to be two things that make her marvel at Jesus. First, here's a man starting a conversation with her, which at first had to seem like he was after the same old thing every guy, religious or not, wants. But the longer she talks to him, the more she realizes he doesn't lust after her but loves her. He's the almost impossibly rare combination of graciousness and purity. Every other guy has either been a gentleman in the name of lust, or completely avoided her in the name of fleeing temptation.

Second, he seems to know everything about her, everything she's ever done, and yet he still loves her. He wants her in a way that has nothing to do with sex yet everything to do with her soul. That's exactly what she goes back to tell the entire town. Come meet a man who told me all that I ever did. Do you hear what she's saying? Come meet a man who knows every last shameful thing I've ever done, yet still wants me. Come meet a man who really knows me, knows all the parts of myself that I hate, and still loves me. Who is like this man?

During my junior year of college, there was a freshman who would agree to anything guys asked. Her pattern was to go to a party, get wasted, and hook up with whoever offered to take her home, sometimes more than one person per party. I saw it happen.

Much like the Samaritan woman, she had a reputation.

Guys loved her, then trashed her as they moved on the next morning. Girls hated her because they saw her as a threat to their boyfriends. Then something happened. Six years after her freshman year, my wife and I ran into her and her husband. She seemed utterly different. As we talked, we learned that she had become a Christian in college, and now she and her husband were headed to seminary to get ready for full-time ministry.

I don't know what she would say if you asked her to tell her story. But I know what happened. She met the same man that a woman much like her met two thousand years before her. A man who didn't want to use her, but wanted her. A man who wasn't interested in shaming her out of her lust, but in loving her out of her lust. A man who could tell her everything she had ever done, yet who loved and forgave her. The only man who, because his love conquers our shame, can conquer our lust and begin to make us new and free from the addictive and destructive patterns of lust we've lived for most of our lives.

And here's the great news: this man said he is the same yesterday, today, and forever. And he still likes to show up in our lives in the very places we're hiding from others because of the pain of our shame. And that's where he will still love us.

9:43 a.m., Friday, October 10, at Drip Coffee

I'M WEARING A SHIRT THAT'S A LITTLE TOO BIG RIGHT now. It's one of my favorite shirts. My sister gave it to me for Christmas last year, which sounds like it wouldn't be a very good shirt. Presents from family are usually like putting a quarter in the gumball machine. Rarely do you get the flavor you want. Also they make you feel as though you're eight years old. Back to the shirt. Rarely do I feel comfortable in my own clothes because rarely do I feel comfortable in my own skin. This shirt is flannel. Construction worker, 1990s chic, which is exactly the vibe I'm going for.

How do you know if lust has become an addiction in your life? And, if it is, what should you do about it? These are two questions I am very much still in the process of exploring. There were countless times before and after becoming a Christian when I swore I would never look at certain things or do certain things again. And there were seasons when I didn't, at least for stretches of time, some of them longer than others.

Looking back now, though, I see there was a common denominator, even in those seasons. I could give up parts of the struggle, say looking at porn, but it was always with the condition that I could hold on to something else, like masturbation. In the words of writer-actor Woody Allen in the movie *Annie Hall*, "Don't knock masturbation. It's sex with someone I love." Masturbation was like an old friend I never wanted to lose touch with.

Early on, just after becoming a Christian as a teenager, I badly wanted to convince myself there was a way of masturbating that was pure. So one Sunday afternoon, I took my Bible into the bathroom, opened it up to Song of Solomon, and tried my best to lust in the purest way. Surprisingly it didn't work. (And now I really hope I reminded my mom not to read this chapter. Mom, if you're reading this, I'm so, so sorry.)

The difference between being a drunk and being a lust drunk is that when you're a drunk, you constantly have to buy and hide a supply stash. When you're a lust drunk, you have one ever present inside you. You might buy subscriptions or videos or magazines or partners. But the lust you get high on is always right there with you, the supply stash in you. This is one of the reasons quitting lust is incredibly hard. It's like quitting drinking while owning a liquor store. It's hard to quit something you have constant access to.

I once confessed my struggle to a pastor, which made me realize how hard it is for students to confess anything to me. He used this illustration to describe how seriously we must fight lust. He said, "Imagine there's a naked woman in my closet at home. I'm going to do everything in my power not to open that closet door. I'm going to put locks on it, board it up, do whatever it takes to keep me from opening that door." Before you call the authorities, or Liam Neeson from *Taken*, know that I recognize that this is a strange illustration. To be fair he was talking about pornography and the deadly serious need to avoid anything and everything that might make you act on your lust.

I agree. Getting rid of the sources of your temptation is an incredibly wise and necessary thing to do if you want to be free of lust. But the way you know it's an addiction is even if you lock the door up as tightly as possible, you still try to get into that closet through the walls or the floors, anything you can do to get a lust fix. More than filters and accountability software, you need to learn a new language, the language of real intimacy. Learning intimacy is like learning French. You absolutely can learn to speak French. And it will take tons of time and practice.

That's the message anyone stuck in the patterns and power of lust needs to hear. Learning to be free of it is as simple and as hard as learning a language. You don't know how to speak the language of true intimacy because you've grown up speaking false intimacy. You know how to speak Lust. You're going to have to learn how to speak Love.

Here's a start. Intimacy and love are more than sex. Much more. When it comes to loving someone, your spouse especially, sex is a small part, not the whole thing. The ABCs of real intimacy involve the communication of longings and fears and dreams, and this makes the awkwardness of honeymoon sex look like a walk in the park.

Learning a new language takes time. A friend in recovery likes to say about change, "Without God, I can't. Without me, God won't." Change is hard; recovery is hard. We want it to be as easy as God taking our lust away, or as simple as following a formula and being forever rid of our lust. It's neither. Change is God working in us as we work to him. God works and we work, his work fueling our work, our work joining his work. Without God, I can't. Without me, God won't. If he had only let "reading" Song of Solomon be my strategy, this whole thing would be much easier.

When I was twenty years old, a friend walked in on me looking at porn. I was living on a fraternity hall at the time, and he had left his book bag in my room. Our resident advisor unlocked the door and let him in the room. It's still among the top five embarrassing moments of my life, right behind being fully pantsed in front of my entire PE class in high school.

The irony is that on the front of that door was the worst sticker I've ever bought. This was around the time when those Calvin and Hobbes stickers that showed Calvin peeing on things were all the rage. This was a Christian version of that. It depicted a more peaceful Calvin, one who had been saved, far from peeing on anything, kneeling at the foot of the cross. Nothing says, "Within these doors lives a great man of God" like putting a Christian sticker on your hall door.

The funny thing is I never once told any of my friends what happened. I immediately got under the covers of my bed and tried my hardest to pretend what had just happened didn't actually happen. That's the way lust goes. Fantasy becomes reality. Then you begin spending your waking moments in denial about the things you've done because you can't bear to be the person that you are. Lust doesn't simply kill love. It eats away your soul. The problem is you are your soul.

Like mushrooms, lust grows best in the dark, unseen, hidden. We have a hard time bringing it into the light. Honesty might be the best policy, but who likes policies? Insurance salesmen maybe, but not us. The kind of honesty we need, first with God and ourselves, then with others, is costly.

I confessed my struggle with lust to my wife when we had been married for almost a year. She found a couple of weird websites in the browsing history on our computer, put things together, and confronted me. One of the first things she said was, "You know I could divorce you, right?" You could have cut the love in that room with that one super dull blade on a Swiss army knife. Did I say love? I meant shame. Because all I could hear was the voice of shame telling me that I would never be enough, never be able to change, never be the kind of husband she could love. That's what shame does. It makes us feel we could never be both known and loved.

My wife would say now that although my struggle with lust affects her in deep and sad ways, she knows my struggle has nothing to do with her. It existed long before I knew her. It's far more about an inability to do intimacy than it is about anything lacking in her. She has been incredibly patient, gracious, and supportive as I learn the language of healthy intimacy and put off sinful patterns that have been part of my life for nearly twenty years.

"Progress, not perfection" is a line we often use. That isn't an excuse not to repent deeply of sexual sin. Instead it's an invitation to see that repenting of sexual sin will take a lifetime for many of us. The good news is that the way Jesus loved his disciples is the way he loves his disciples still: to the end.

There's a scene in the movie *Traffic* where Michael Douglas finds out his daughter is addicted to crack and she's gone missing. So Douglas goes looking for her, knocking on every door he knows to knock on, talking to every one of her friends he can think to talk to, until he finally finds the dealer who's been selling crack to her. He confronts the dealer and pushes open the door. There is his daughter, high, writhing on the bed, a strange older man beside her pulling his pants up and leaving. As you watch the scene, the thought pounding in your heart is what is the father going to do?

This is what he does. He kneels beside the bed and begins to cry as he kisses her on the cheek. Then he lifts her into his arms and takes her home. Every time I watch that scene, I get a glimpse of the way Jesus has loved me.

C. S. Lewis wrote about how God shows grace like this. "If God were proud He would hardly have us on such terms: but He is not proud, He stoops to conquer, He will have us even though we have shown that we prefer everything else to Him, and come to Him because there is 'nothing better' now to be had."[9]

The Lord loves to love people out of their lust in ways that begin to transform them from the inside out. No earthly love can bring about the kind of purity we need. But there is a love waiting to lead us into a life of reality, one that makes our lust-filled secret world of isolation pale by comparison.

Chapter Five

D IS ALSO FOR DEPRESSION

1:48 p.m., Friday, October 17, at Drip Coffee

I JUST GOT BACK FROM A RECOVERY MEETING, AND IT was super encouraging. We were talking to a potential new friend in the fellowship about how easy it is to wear the mask of togetherness, especially in ministry positions. The mask of togetherness maybe hints at having a past but gets defensive and dishonest about any struggling that might be present tense. We all have a past. Yes. But we all have a present too. Ways we're hiding the truth from ourselves and from others. Ways we're falling short while pretending to walk tall. It's funny how much writing a book about vulnerability makes you realize you're not vulnerable. I read the other day on Twitter about the difference between transparency and vulnerability. (I see the irony.) I can be transparent all day long because I want you to like me. Being vulnerable, on the other hand, is harder because I don't want you to be able to hurt me. Transparency is as different from vulnerability as wedding pictures are from a real marriage. One looks good; the other requires entrusting your life to another. Transparency is good for the image. Vulnerability is good for the soul.

When I was twenty-one, I carefully placed a suicide note where I knew my girlfriend would find it and slinked off into the night of my hometown with no thought other than a nagging desire to end it all. It wasn't the first time in my life when I wanted to kill myself, but it was the first time when I wanted those close to me to know that I wanted to kill myself. It was a cry for help. More like a full-blown Howard Dean scream for help. Suicidal thoughts certainly weren't new to me. They started around the time my parents split up. But I had never been this close to actually acting on them before.

How did I get to that point? That's a question I've often asked. Am I depressed because I made poor choices, or did I make poor choices because I'm depressed? Which came first: the chicken or the egg? Did they both end up dying sad, lonely deaths at a dirty KFC in a small southern town? Probably.

The reality is that the answer to the questions above—not the chicken question—is probably yes. Yes, I was depressed because I made poor choices. And yes, I made bad choices because I was depressed. Some of these bad choices may or may not have included a late-night visit to

KFC, when I ordered a "family meal" for one. And then I ate my family. My delicious, delicious family.

Some people major in business in college. I majored in depression. I remember going to see a therapist and telling him that most days I could barely find the strength to get out of bed and make it to class. I'll never forget his response. He said, "It's easy. Just swing your feet onto the floor and get up." I definitely broke the sixth commandment in my heart that day. (The one that says, "Thou shalt not kill your therapist.") If only getting over depression were as easy as he said.

The reality is that at some point in our lives everyone gets depressed. You might struggle with clinical depression that comes and goes in frustrating and unpredictable waves. If not, you will at some point wrestle with circumstantial depression. Life will disappoint you, even devastate you. The natural human response is to get depressed about it, maybe put on a little Bon Iver and some sweatpants, then curl into a ball for a few days (or weeks).

If depression is something you and I will eventually experience in one form or another, why is it still so awkward to talk about? Talking about it openly and without shame ought to be one of the key ways to fight depression. So why do we not talk about it? Because like most things that make us feel awkward, there are no easy answers. We like to talk about things we feel we have answers for, but what about those things that raise more questions than answers? Even a cursory reading of those psalms where David is really depressed tells us that he felt very, very alone in his sadness because his friends didn't know what to do with it.

I once had a conversation over frozen yogurt with a severely depressed friend. We had both just graduated from college and were living back home for the summer (we call both of those significant depression triggers). The tide had started to turn on my depression, and I was feeling pretty good, and so my friend wanted to talk about how I had gotten better. At that point my understanding of my own depression was still simplistic, and I had no idea it would come back with a vengeance in my mid-twenties. So when she asked me the question, "How did you get over your depression?" I remember simply saying, "Jesus," as I spooned some more TCBY in my mouth. I'm sure she wanted to punch me in the face.

Looking back I should have said something like, "You know, I'm not exactly sure, but I think working a landscaping job, eating more of Mom's home-cooked meals, and getting involved in the church again have started to help." The point is that if someone who's depressed can't have a helpful conversation with a friend who's depressed, imagine how many awkward, unhelpful conversations are happening between a depressed friend and those friends who can't relate at all.

Talking about depression is also difficult because we have different ideas about why we get depressed in the first place. Whenever we start talking about depression, we are typically talking about three different aspects: the spiritual, the emotional, and the physical. To deal with only one of these elements is to reduce depression to something that can be easily managed. But taking all three aspects seriously means there can be no simplistic answers. My depression may be *mainly* rooted in one of them, but rarely is it *solely* rooted in one of them.

The spiritual component of depression means that sometimes depression is rooted in sinful choices. You and I get depressed because we choose what God asks us not to choose or fail to choose what he asks us to choose. Like David in Psalm 32, the answer to this kind of depression isn't to cover up our sin, but to confess it and seek the grace we need to repent.

We need safe people in our lives, pastors especially, who understand their own sinfulness enough to be gentle, but who also have experienced God's grace enough to be hopeful about themselves, though they know they will never have it all together. This makes them quick to listen and slow to speak, the kind of friends you desperately need when you're depressed because they don't make you feel crazy for not getting better as quickly as other people think you should.

The emotional component of depression means that sometimes our depression is rooted in the ways we've been sinned against. We get depressed because we experience the brokenness of life. Parents get divorced. Friends die of cancer. We lose a relationship that means the world to us. Like Luke Skywalker in *The Empire Strikes Back*, we get depressed because life isn't exactly going our way. If only Yoda were available for counseling. All of us have places where we've hurt others, and all of us have places where we ourselves have been hurt. Good counselors help us face the way our past has shaped us, and the way we shape our presents in order to deal with the difficulties of life.

The physical component of depression is the most controversial in Christian circles. Unfortunately Jesus didn't work anything about antidepressants into the Sermon on the Mount. It's a gray area, something we typically don't handle well in Christendom. Mentioning antidepressants in some churches is like wearing a Red Sox hat at Yankee Stadium: you could do it, but please don't. But is it possible that I'm depressed because something is physically wrong in my brain?

The longer I've studied and dealt with my family's history of depression, the more I'm convinced that it certainly can have a physical cause. If my kidney can get sick, why can't my brain get sick? This means medicine may be as helpful as both repentance and counseling. We need good doctors in our lives, doctors who treat a prescription pad with the same carefulness Batman treats his utility belt. You don't whip out the grappling hook in every situation, but you're not afraid to use it in the right situations either.

Antidepressants aren't a magic bullet, but they can be unbelievably helpful. Martin Luther, who was prone to deep depression, said, "When I was ill . . . the physicians made me take as much medicine as though I had been a great bull. . . . I do not deny that medicine is a gift of God, nor do I refuse to acknowledge science in the skill of many physicians; but, take the best of them, how far are they from perfection?"[1]

2:25 p.m., Sunday, October 19, at my house

TRIED TO GO WRITE AT A LOCAL COFFEE SHOP, BUT IT was full of people, and people are the worst. In the words of my friend, "I'm not a people person, I'm an only-certain-people person." So I opted to come back to a Starbucks on this side of town. As I pulled into a parking spot, my wife called and, fighting back tears of parental failure and rage, told me our eight-year-old son just said the "F word." Sometimes being a parent feels like being dropped in a corn maze with no map, no guide, and very little hope you'll ever make it out. Also there are little monsters everywhere. So I rushed back home, ready to wash his mouth out with soap, only to get a second call saying there was a slight misunderstanding. He didn't say the full "F word." He just said "I 'F-word' you" to his sister because she wouldn't play the game he wanted to play on the trampoline. Now I'm less worried about my son cussing and more worried that he's going to be bad at it. So now I'm writing at home while lying in my bed, just like Winston Churchill.

Martyn Lloyd-Jones was a pastor in London in the 1960s. He was a physician before being called into ministry, and as a result, he often counseled many depressed people in his congregation. This was his warning to fellow Christians:

> Many Christian people, in fact, are in utter ignorance concerning this realm where the borderlines between the physical, psychological and spiritual meet. Frequently I have found that such [church] leaders had treated those whose trouble was obviously mainly physical or psychological, in a purely spiritual manner; and if you do so, you not only don't help. You aggravate the problem.[2]

Dr. Lloyd-Jones knew that to begin to help a depressed person you have to deal with them as a whole person: body, soul, and mind. We need the help of pastors, counselors, and doctors. But we also need a better grasp on what depression feels like so we'll know it when we see it.

The best description of depression I've ever read is from Darlene Withers, a character in Jeffrey Eugenides's novel *The Marriage Plot*. She's at an Alcoholics Anonymous meeting describing the difference between addiction and depression: "One thing I learned, between addiction and depression? Depression a lot worse. Depression ain't something you just get *off* of. You can't get clean from depression. Depression be like a bruise that never goes away. A bruise in your mind. You just got to be careful not to touch where it hurts. It always be there, though."[3]

The thing I've noticed about a bruise is sometimes you know what caused it, and sometimes you look down and have a little dark bluish spot on your arm and you have no idea where it came from. I once had a counselor tell me that depression always has its roots in sin, and he found that hopeful because it meant you could always do something to make it go away. I sat across the booth from him at Ruby Tuesday, quietly listening as I ate my chicken fingers, thinking that maybe my depression had its roots in the fact that I'm eating at Ruby Tuesday, the Crocs with khakis of the restaurant world.

What if depression isn't so much a choice as it is a condition that both includes and influences our choices? Novelist David Foster Wallace imagined depression as "The Bad

Thing," a dark monster that "tears you open and gets in there and squirms around . . . [and] not only attacks you and makes you feel bad and puts you out of commission, it especially attacks and makes you feel bad and puts out of commission precisely those things that are necessary in order for you to fight the Bad Thing, to maybe get better, to stay alive."[4]

Kind of like that Smoke Monster in *Lost*, but worse because it's inside you, installing the viral software of hopelessness and shame into the operating system that is your mind. (But then maybe we're all depressed because of how disappointing the *Lost* finale was. I think David Foster Wallace would have agreed.)

If we're comparing depression to bruises, another interesting similarity is that even though bruises have to heal from the inside out, there are some things you can do to help that healing process. Like ice. And massages (not at the same time). At least that's what Wikipedia tells me, and I trust Wikipedia like I trust our cat: not at all.

The point is there are some things that we can do not only to break the cycle of depression but also to help the healing process (which typically lasts a lifetime). For me those things have included: eating less fast food and more whole foods, jogging, getting out of my head, getting together with friends, watching lots of Netflix with my wife, counseling, counseling, and counseling. Did I mention counseling? Okay, good. Because that's important.

None of these things will fix you, of course. After all, you're a human being, not a laptop. You can fix laptops, but you can't fix human beings. Instead you have to do the hard work of learning to love yourself the way God loves you. You have a heart, not a hard drive. If you had to be a laptop, though, hopefully you'd be a Mac and not a PC. Judging by your jeans, you're probably a PC.

The thing about bruises is you need to be gentle with them. The initial damage has been done, and they continue to hurt. But God is gentle with us in the very places where we are often hardest on ourselves. In fact, he promises not to break a reed that is badly bruised (Isa. 42:3), but instead to gently restore it until it is strong enough to stand again. If depression is like a bruise, then God's love is like a balm, which soothes and restores. It's not a quick fix, but something gently applied over the course of a lifetime.

One of the cruelest things about depression is that you genuinely believe no one could really like you, much less love you. This belief is not only the root of those forced and clumsy interactions you have with others, but it's also what makes being depressed really, really devastating. Author and therapist Ed Welch has described this phenomenon in the article "Depression's Odd Filter":

> Someone says to you, "I love you."
>
> You hear . . . nothing. Actually you hear something. You hear a little voice in your brain that says, "I'm worthless. You're only saying you love me because you think you have to."
>
> Somehow, from the mouths of other people to your ear, all words of blessing and encouragement get tumbled upside down and backward and confirm your suspicions

about yourself. You are an abject failure. Unloved. Unlovable. And everyone knows it.

There are hundreds of variations.

"You look nice today."

Push it through the filter of depression and you get, "Not true. I know I am ugly."

Or, "You seem to be feeling a little better today."

This means, "Oh, you don't want to talk to me anymore."

This is your brain on depression. And we could add, it is your brain on shame.[5]

To me this is still the hardest part about depression, to be unable to hear or accept love from anyone. To have your mind twist every comment and interaction. Earlier this year I was feeling particularly rejected by a friend, so I did what most depressed people do and wrote him a really long passive-aggressive e-mail. I was mainly upset that he had turned down a dinner invitation—you know, like a normal human being who has a life outside of a friendship with just one person. His response was incredibly gracious.

One thing he said particularly stood out to me. He wrote, "Can I just go on record and say that I like you?" This was huge because he was saying I will do everything in my power to assure you that I like being your friend, regardless of what your thoughts and feelings are telling you.

When you're depressed, it's like you pick up one of those shields in a video game, but instead of protecting your life power, it blocks you from being able to receive any affirmation or encouragement. No matter what someone says, or how they say it, you don't believe them. You can't believe them, no matter how hard you try. But, speaking for the depressed, let me go on record and say that we need you to keep trying. We need you to fight for friendship with us even when we can barely lift a finger to call you back, much less get out of bed for the day. We need you to believe our friendship is worth fighting for even if it seems we've given up completely ourselves.

Sometimes the need is simple, to be with us in the midst of our sadness, because the last thing people who are really depressed need is to talk about why they're really depressed. But this isn't a sign that we don't want others around. We desperately do. We just want and need someone to embrace the awkward silence with us. It's okay to sit in silence because life is hard and nobody has all the answers.

There's a scene in the movie *Lars and the Real Girl* that I love. Lars (played by Ryan Gosling) has just lost his pretend "girlfriend" Bianca (a life-size doll), and the community (who's been playing along) comes over to grieve with him at her "death." They treat it like a real funeral and bring food to the house after. And as they do, one of the older women from the church says, "That's what you do when people get sad. Bring casseroles and sit." I'm afraid most of us aren't very good at sitting.

One of the best and simplest ways to fight depression is with humor. A friend of mine went to see a pastor about the severe depression that he was experiencing. As he walked through the church halls, undoubtedly he thought the pastor would say something to the effect of "You need to _____ more." Pray. Repent. Read your Bible. The pastor's prescription, however, shocked him. He said, "What I want you to do is buy the complete collection of *Seinfeld*, then watch two episodes every night before bed with your roommates."

He knew a secret. My friend later learned that the pastor had wrestled with severe depression too. And he had learned to fight it with laughter.

I've been told that Martin Luther was once depressed to the point of spending entire days in bed, so his wife, Katharine, dressed herself in all black and put on a veil. When Luther asked her whose funeral she was going to, she said, "God's, because the way you're acting is so hopeless he must be dead." She understood that humor is a vital part of dealing with depression, because if you listen closely enough to laughter you can hear the echoes of hope.

That's what depressed people need more than anything: the gift of laughing at themselves. Because within that gift is another hidden gift: the realization that things aren't as bad as they seem, and that they will not go on this way forever.

I know it's not easy to love a depressed person, being one myself. If you're depressed, you can navigate some of this awkwardness by helping your friends and family understand what you're going through and what you need. I've put some thoughts together that you can easily (and, if you prefer, passive-aggressively) share with friends. They'll love you more effectively and better understand what you're going through.

1. *Keep the pin in the shame grenade.* Depressed people feel tremendous amounts of shame. The voice they hear

most often in their head is like the anti-Robin Williams in *Good Will Hunting*: "It's your fault. It's your fault. It's your fault." The problem is not that they don't know what they should do. The problem is finding the strength to do it. They're carrying a heavy load. Don't be the kind of friend who adds to it. Be the kind of friend who helps lighten it. Don't patronize; empathize. In the words of Brené Brown, "Empathy's the antidote to shame."[6]

2. *Don't be simplistic.* Nothing is worse than treating depression simplistically. It's not always as simple as "take medicine" or "go see a counselor" or "repent" (usually all three will be part of the healing process). To make one of those the "end all, be all" is extremely unhelpful. Help the depressed person simplify things, yes. But don't be simplistic.

3. *Take the physical as seriously as the spiritual.* Depressed people probably aren't looking for another book (except for *this* book—you should definitely give them this one). Give them a steak instead, preferably an expensive one. And pair it with a loaded baked potato and, if you want to get really spiritual, a whole pan of Sister Schubert rolls. That's what God did for Elijah when he was depressed to the point of wanting life to be over. He didn't give him a lecture or even a devotional. He gave him a meal and then let him sleep (1 Kings 19:4–7). He didn't "Jesus juke" him, to use writer Jon Acuff's phrase, by shaming him for not being "spiritual" enough. In fact, he took the physical just as seriously as the spiritual. Because sometimes the most spiritual thing a depressed person can do is take a nap (or a walk, or a meal).

4. *Embrace awkward silence.* If depressed people could take a book title for a life motto, it would be *More Baths, Less Talking* (Nick Hornby). That's good because you know that with the number of baths they've probably taken, depressed people are really clean. Sometimes all that's needed is presence, to just be with someone without looking for or requiring anything in return. At the very least, this will mean minimal awkward conversations while still communicating powerfully. Give them the gift of embracing with them the painfully awkward silence without making them feel awkward for it.

5. *Help them take themselves less seriously.* The last word you'd use about being around a depressed person is *fun.* That's because everything feels so sad and serious when you're depressed. So one of the best things you can do for a depressed person is to help him take himself less seriously. "Angels can fly because they can take themselves lightly,"[7] according to G. K. Chesterton.

6. *Give them grace by giving them space.* Depressed people need the space to be alone, yet with the security that you're not going anywhere. Don't get all up in their grill. Be content to hang out on their back porch while they're inside on the couch watching their seventh episode in a row of *New Girl.* They need the space of you leaving them alone, with the grace of knowing you'll never leave them.

8:58 a.m., Monday, October 20, at Drip Coffee

I DON'T FEEL LIKE WRITING TODAY (SHOCKER), BUT I'M going to because I've been given a gob of time because I'm not preaching this week. Today is already very Monday-y for a

Monday. My wife and I got into a fight about money. The kids need some new winter clothes because they're doing that thing where they keep growing every year. I wish money were like Ryan Gosling, something you don't have to think about unless you want to, and when you do it is pure, warm, fuzzy goodness. Most marriages involve a saver and a spender. Not ours. Two spenders got together in this one. It's a party until the money runs out, and then it's a knock-down, drag-out game of Battleship, trying to pinpoint where the other person over-spent so you can sink their argument Battleship. All I want to do instead of thinking about money or writing is watch last night's episode of *Walking Dead*. Come to think of it, writing feels a lot like killing zombies—impossible until you do it.

One of the books of Scripture I'm most thankful for is Psalms. You can't read the psalms and miss that having a relationship with God is often painful, sometimes sad, and most times messier than we wish. In particular I'm thankful for what scholars over the years have identified as the lament psalms. These are the psalms that sound similar to the melancholy tracks on your favorite Coldplay album. They're sad. Really sad. And they aren't afraid to bring that sadness to God and even direct it toward him.

Psalm 42 fits into that category. We're not sure exactly who wrote it. All we really know is the writer seems to be coming from a place of deep loneliness, a foreign land where he never wanted to live. Some people call this college. Others, the South. Still others, Canada. As you read what he wrote, you get the feeling he really misses home.

It is also unmistakable how sad he feels. He describes his depression vividly. It feels like dying of thirst (verses 1–2), eating at a buffet of tears (verse 3), listening to an inner critic on a loop (verses 3 and 10), being emptied out like a leftover drink at a party (verse 4), feeling nostalgia for sad things (verse 4), drowning in the ocean (verse 7), and having a fatal wound in your bones (verse 10). You have to give depressed people credit for being obsessively detailed and thorough about why being alive is the worst.

If you can take all these images and hold them together in one word, it would simply be *hopeless*. You feel hopeless about yourself. Hopeless about others. Hopeless about life. Hopeless about the future. Hopeless about the past. Hopeless about the present. Hopeless about God.

One of my favorite scenes in David Foster Wallace's *Infinite Jest* takes place in a cold room in a psych ward between a doctor and Kate Gompert, who's recently tried to kill herself again by taking an insane amount of pills. The doctor asks her why she wants to kill herself, and what she says is stunningly insightful:

> No matter what I do it gets worse and worse, it's there more and more, this filter drops down, and the feeling makes the fear of the feeling way worse, and after a couple weeks it's there all the time, the feeling, and I'm totally inside it, I'm in it and everything has to pass through it to get in, and I don't want to smoke [pot], and I don't want to work, or go out, or read, or watch [TV], or go out, or stay in, or either do anything or not

do anything, I don't want *anything* except for the feeling
to go *away*. But it doesn't. Part of the feeling is being like
willing to do anything to make it go away. Understand
that. *Anything.* Do you understand? It's not wanting to
hurt myself it's wanting to *not hurt*.[8]

That's exactly what I was feeling the night I almost
killed myself. Hopeless and wanting not to hurt anymore.
I didn't know it at the time, but this is precisely the place
the Lord met me. He loves to bring hope to the hopeless.
Sometimes that hope comes flooding. Most times it slowly
fills those whose hearts ache with sadness. In my case, it's
been much more of the latter.

Every summer I get to stand up in front of a group of
a couple of hundred college students and share about my
struggle with depression. And every year without fail, as I
get to the end of our time together, there's one thought that
always brings me to tears. Even as I'm writing about it outside on these new lounge couches at Starbucks, I'm fighting
back tears. The thought is simply this: as hard as going
through the darkness of depression has been, the Lord has
not gone anywhere but has stayed by my side even in my
lowest moments.

The image that always comes to my mind is that of Jesus
praying in the Garden of Gethsemane the night before his
death on the cross. All his friends have let him down, he's
full of anxiety, and his Father feels a million miles away.
Yet he pushes further into the darkness, through the night,
to the ultimate darkness of condemnation, separation,

shame, and even death itself. This means that in my darkest moments, I'm not without the presence of one who understands my darkness, or the hope of one who already faced it on my behalf. He's with me in the darkness and he's for me through the darkness.

This is why "Poor Sinner, Dejected with Fear," is my favorite hymn in the world. It was written by the nineteenth-century English pastor William Gadsby, and has been sung by depressed and anxious people all over the world for some two hundred years now.

> *Poor sinner, dejected with fear,*
> *Unbosom thy mind to the Lamb;*
> *No wrath on His brow He does wear,*
> *Nor will He poor mourners condemn;*
> *His arm of omnipotent grace*
> *Is able and willing to save;*
> *A sweet and a permanent peace*
> *He'll freely and faithfully give.*

The bad news is that most times our depression won't ever just magically go away. The good news is that no matter how bad our depression gets, we're in the care of a Great Physician who promises to never go away. Now let's go eat our family at KFC.

Chapter Six

I KISSED MARRIAGE HELLO AFTER KISSING DATING GOODBYE

10:13 a.m., Thursday, October 30, at Drip Coffee

I'VE BEEN AVOIDING WRITING FOR A SOLID HOUR NOW, so long that my coffee is that undrinkable kind of cold. Don't get me wrong; I'm still drinking it, like a good addict. I think I'm depressed. When you're sad even after working out at a quarter to six in the morning, you're probably depressed. But I'm afraid to get back on Lexapro for two reasons. Number one, I'm afraid it will dry up my creative juices and turn me into a happy zombie. Number two, I'm afraid it will make me gain weight. I just bought these thirty-four-inch jeans and I can't afford new thirty-sixes. I also can't afford looking in the mirror and getting even more depressed. Maybe I'm in denial about my need to be back on medicine. A depressed person probably isn't the best judge of whether he should be on it. These jeans are tight. I wish I meant that in the rapper sense. I don't.

My wife and I got married on a cold, rainy December day in 2003, so we decided for our honeymoon we would escape to a tropical destination. We chose one of those all-inclusive retreats in Jamaica. Nothing like celebrating being newly married by secluding yourself in a gated resort after driving through hours and hours of people living in crushing poverty.

This newly married tropical adventure came with two huge mistakes on my part, the first before we left and the other while we were there. The first might still be my favorite. In preparing for the fun and sun of Jamaica, I went to a tanning bed for the first time in my life. Remember, it was December. I was reaching the paleness of *Twilight*'s Edward Cullen, and who wants to have honeymoon sex looking like a vampire? Other than *Twilight* fans.

I waltzed into the tanning salon with the confidence of a soon-to-be golden god. When the gentleman working the tanning bed (read: running some kind of money laundering ring) asked me how long I wanted to tan, I told him fifteen minutes. Fifteen minutes in the sun? Safe. Fifteen minutes in a tanning bed? Nightmare.

To fully understand how badly this went, you must also know two key facts. One, in preparation for honeymoon sex, I completely shaved the trunk of my body, because who wants to have sex with a werewolf? Besides those *Twilight* fans, I mean. Two, I went fully naked into the tanning bed, except for the little goggles they give you to put over your eyes.

I went home, feeling a little crispy. Took a nap. Woke up, feeling like I'd been rotated in a microwave, looked in the mirror and gasped. Did I mention this was the day before our wedding? When I showed up at the rehearsal, my wife saw me and immediately burst into tears. If you ever come to my house, you'll notice all our wedding pictures are in black and white. This is why. The few in color make me look like the offspring of a hotdog and a raccoon.

The second thing that happened on this tropical honeymoon that's already off to a bad start is this. Neither my wife nor I was very experienced when it came to sex. All I really knew was what I had seen in movies. For both of us there was a steep learning curve, and I encountered mine pretty quickly.

When we arrived in our room the first night, a bottle of champagne was chilling for us. The chilling part is key to this story. After showering off the beach sand, we moved to the bed for a night of romance. Without any warning I grabbed the bottle of champagne, popped the cork, and poured half of it on my wife. Just like in movies. And by "in movies," I probably mean porn.

Doesn't every woman dream of having her new, sexy, hairless, hotdog-tanned husband pour ice-cold champagne on her to spice things up in the bedroom? Turns out nope. Not at all. My wife's response, and I quote, was "What the h— are you doing?" When you get the word "h—" out of a good Southern Baptist girl, you know you are messing up something colossally. I was.

The Dowager Countess on *Downton Abbey* got it right when she said, "Everyone goes down the aisle with half the story hidden." Mine included a completely unrealistic view of sex. Also of women and of how things work in general.

Our problem when it comes to relationships, especially romantic ones, is typically that we don't know what we know, and we think we know what we don't know. Whenever I marry a couple, I tell them I'm a much bigger believer in postmarital counseling than I am in premarital counseling. Whenever you tell a couple something in premarital counseling, they pretend to listen. It's not until they get into marriage and get good and disappointed that they're actually ready to listen and willing to understand.

The same goes for dating. A counselor told a very depressed, just-gone-through-a-devastating-breakup me that what my girlfriend and I felt for each other wasn't really love, it was infatuation. I wanted to punch him in his bespectacled face, but I lacked the strength because of depression. It wasn't until I met my wife that I had a clue what he was talking about, or the ability to emotionally accept the truth of it.

The best thing about the invention of a time machine would be the ability for future-us to constantly go back to now-us and reveal all the things we're missing, all the things we don't know and can't know. Maybe then we would have a shot at entering relationships with a desire and ability to be healthy in them. Instead we come in like a new player in the video game Halo. No matter how many times we're killed, we rush in to make the same mistakes, only to be killed again. We then throw the controller down, wondering why we keep getting killed so fast.

Perhaps the biggest mistake we make in romantic relationships is to mistake a feeling for love, and to mistake love for a feeling.

A single friend and I were talking about marriage the other day. He's afraid of marriage because he's worried about getting ten years into it and realizing he badly wants out, of waking up one day hating the life he chose and, more specifically, the person he chose to marry.

Behind our fear of commitment is a fear of being unhappy. Isn't the point of marriage, the thinking goes, to make me happier than I would be if I weren't married? And if I'm not happier, then wouldn't it be better to tap out, to put the marriage down quietly like a beloved golden retriever who made us happy for as long as he could but now is dying?

What's interesting is that the fear of being unhappy lies behind the fear of being single. I will finally be happy once I'm married, the thinking goes. Then life will really begin. Until then I'm just wasting time trying to meet, awkwardly side hug, date, awkwardly front hug, then marry the right person, preferably meeting them at a church event so I know they're a "good" guy or girl. Because we all know that only good guys and girls go to church, and if a guy or girl goes to church, they're obviously good.

Wanting happiness isn't a bad thing. It's a human thing. The problem is that happiness is less something we can directly seek than it is a by-product of seeking the right things in the right ways. Happiness is like the endorphins that flow after a good workout. They're a result of hunting another goal, not something you can get your hands on directly. They only come by working out. Or so I hear. I'm less a work-out guy, more a work-in guy. And by that I mean most days I like to work on getting an entire bag of chips inside me.

Jesus told us to "seek first the kingdom of God and his righteousness, and all these things will be added to you" (Matt. 6:33). Blessings, like happiness, come as we focus our eyes on something other than those blessings. Jesus is teaching us here to think less like consumers and more like himself, a covenant-making and covenant-keeping God. If Jesus had let happiness determine his choices, the cross would have never happened. Jesus' choices were driven by his covenant promises, first to God, then to us.

If we approach marriage as consumers, then getting married will feel like buying a new iPhone. It's really exciting at first, but then it gets old, and we convince ourselves that we would be happier if we had a new iPhone. Or maybe it'd be better to switch to a Galaxy? And so spouses go from persons we've made promises to, to products that exist to make our lives easier and help us feel better about ourselves.

Additionally, conflict in marriage becomes a flaw, a glitch in the system, that means the marriage isn't working as it should. The product is obviously defective, and you don't keep a defective product. You return it for a new one. The last thing you do is keep it.

But the foundation of marriage, laid down at the

beginning of the world, is the idea of covenant. In a covenant, I make vows, deep promises, that no matter what happens or how things turn out, I will be here, stay here, and love you. And a no-matter-what kind of love is the kind of love we all crave. Marriage is the only relationship in which this kind of love can go from being a dream to a reality. I love what theologian and ethicist Lewis Smedes said about marriage: "My wife has lived with at least five different men since we were wed—and each of the five has been me."[1]

Covenant love loves through all the changing seasons of a person's life, the falls, winters, springs, and summers. The winter might be cold and long, but it's worth waiting for the fresh blooms of spring.

Having covenant in the back of your mind means conflict isn't an unwelcome flaw; instead it's evidence that your spouse is another person. You didn't marry yourself. You married someone else, who has different dreams, different fears, different desires, different struggles, different interests, and a different personality from yours. This conflict has the potential to polish you, sharpen you, mold you, and refine you into being a much more lovelier and wholehearted person than you could ever be without it.

Several years ago *Saturday Night Live* did a parody of the dating website eHarmony, called meHarmony. The idea was simple but brilliant: each character married the opposite sex version of themselves. At one point Kenan Thompson's character said, "I didn't think it was possible to meet someone who loves me as much as I love me!"

If we're being honest, this is exactly how we wish things

would go in marriage. Loving yourself comes easy. Loving another person is hard work. By definition to love someone else means giving up loving yourself. I don't mean abandoning the kind of self-love (or self-care) that is healthy and good and necessary to healthy relationships. The math of marriage is "one whole person plus one whole person equals one healthy marriage."

To love someone else means to put that person before yourself, not in a way that lets him or her control you or run all over you, but in a way that invites a sacrificial self-denial in return. Two people sacrificially loving and serving each other in this way is like magic: very few people believe it could possibly exist until they see for themselves.

This kind of mutual sacrifice and service is exactly the kind of love God has for us. The Father's love led him to give his Son for us. The Son's love led him to give himself for us. The Spirit's love leads him to shine a spotlight on the love of the Father and the Son. This same love leads us to give ourselves first to him and, in turn, to each other.

The good news of the gospel is that God didn't wait for us to love him before he loved us. He made a covenant with us to be our God, and his favorite picture of that covenant is marriage. He loves marriage so much he even calls himself a husband, and his people his wife. It's a love that never fails to pursue, to move toward, to serve, and to lead.

The problem in this marriage with God is that we haven't been a faithful spouse. We've loved ourselves more than we've loved God. We've proven over and over that we prefer almost anything to him. We favor our plans to his plans, our will to his will. We even make god-substitutes of people, places, and things. We've been deeply unfaithful. As Tim Keller puts it: "God is in the longest-lived, worst marriage in the history of the world."[2]

Yet he is a faithful husband. If he were a consumer, he would have traded us in or returned us a long time ago. But he isn't. He is a covenant-making, covenant-keeping God. He would sooner die himself than break a single one of his promises to us.

Marriage is two people, who should have given up on each other a long time ago, not giving up on each other. Marriage is still the best picture of the gospel.

11:27 a.m., Friday, October 31, at Starbucks

BEFORE I SAT DOWN I ASKED THE BARISTA SERVING ME if they did French presses anymore. She looked at me like I was hurting her and then said, "No." Those two letters, when put together and floated in my direction, don't sit well with me. They lie down all over the couch of my heart and put their dirty feet up. One day maybe I'll be mature enough for someone to tell me no, and I won't have to hold back my face like it's a guy about to get into a bar fight. But do I think that day will be any time soon? No.

But marriage isn't the only picture of the gospel. Singleness captures the love of God in a beautiful way too. Jesus himself was single. So have been many of his disciples, like Paul, for example. Far from being a curse, singleness is just as much of a blessing as marriage.

Sometimes the church talks about singleness as if it were similar to being chosen for HufflePuff by the Magic Sorting Hat in *Harry Potter*. The good news is that you still are at Hogwarts, but the bad news is that pretty much everyone else there will avoid you and make it clear they feel sad for you and would never, ever want to be you.

Somewhere along the way someone decided it would be good to start calling it "the gift of singleness," which actually is pretty accurate given that most of the gifts I've ever gotten were not something I wanted and something I wish I could return. That's how many of us feel about singleness.

The most common thing we hear about singleness is that it's something you're called to. This sounds kind of scary, like the call that is less your best friend calling to ask how a date went and more the one coming from inside the house in a horror movie.

The idea of "calling" is twofold, external and internal. Internally you feel drawn. Externally you feel confirmed. Singleness, when put in those terms, would be something you actually wanted and also something others could see as potentially good for you. It goes from being a curse to being a blessing. Some of God's greatest gifts to the church are singles who love the freedom to serve that their singleness affords them.

This also means singleness is something we are all called to, at least for part of our lives. Knowing God's goodness to us in singleness, and the blessings he has for us unique to it, moves singleness from being a season we endure to a season we enjoy. Instead of a mark of shame, it becomes a sign of grace.

Paige Benton Brown, a former chaplain at Vanderbilt University, reflected on God's goodness to her in her singleness:

> Can God be any less good to me on the average Tuesday morning than he was on that monumental Friday afternoon when he hung on a cross in my place? The answer is a resounding NO. God will not be less good to me tomorrow either, because God cannot be less good to me. His goodness is not the effect of his disposition but the essence of his person—not an attitude but an attribute.
>
> I long to be married. My younger sister got married two months ago. She now has an adoring husband, a beautiful home, a whirlpool bathtub, and all-new Corningware. Is God being any less good to me than he is to her? The answer is a resounding NO. God will not be less good to me because God cannot be less good to me. It is a cosmic impossibility for God to shortchange any of his children. God can no more live in me apart from the perfect fullness of his goodness and grace than I can live in Nashville and not be white. If he fluctuated one quark in his goodness, he would cease to be God."[3]

God never promises us marriage. Nor does he promise us singleness. What he does promise us is himself. He promises that whatever it is he calls us to, however hard, however long, he will never cease being good to us. This is the secret to happiness: knowing that my life is in his hands and because of that he holds good things for me. And when bad things do come, and they will, that he will never stop holding me.

When I was fifteen years old, just before my freshman year of high school, I became a Christian. In one sense it wasn't dramatic at all. In another it turned my whole life upside down, especially when it came to girls. Suddenly my heart was no longer set on having a girlfriend. I was pretty content, actually strangely content, just to be a youth group kid. If you weren't a youth group kid, imagine the best party you ever went to in high school, take out all the things that probably made it fun, and replace them with Disney movies, chubby bunnies, and a plethora of 1980s and '90s dance music.

Then something happened: my best friend got a girlfriend. He was also a youth group kid, and so was his girlfriend. I looked at them, looked back at myself, and decided it was time for me to find a girlfriend, because obviously what God does in someone else's life he must do in mine, too, especially when it comes to romance.

It only made sense that I would pursue the friend of my best friend's new girlfriend. Was she a youth group girl? Check. She didn't cuss? Check. She didn't drink? Check. She bowed her head and said a blessing at school before lunch? Double check. Just like the Proverbs 31 woman.

Little did I know how desperate my heart was for someone who would know me and love me to the end. If I could go back, I would try to tell seventeen-year-old me that maybe the best person to love you like that isn't a fifteen-year-old girl. I probably wouldn't have listened. It's hard to hear when you're busy tightening your matching WWJD bracelets while listening to your favorite Christian ska bands.

The telling moment that things were about to be unhealthy was after a second date. We had finished eating at Applebee's. (A story should only get better when it begins with eating at Applebee's. This one didn't.) As we got back into the car, I gave her a card I had bought earlier that day. In that card I had written the three little words we all long to hear (besides "I ordered pizza"). I remember her face as she read the words, "I love you." Her expression was somewhere between "squirrel trying to cross the road" and "dog getting too close to the electric fence."

The crazy thing is four months after that we began dating for real. From the start everyone knew we should break up, but we were stubborn and fought it. Hard. Fittingly, our relationship started the same time Josh Harris wrote his classic book on relationships, *I Kissed Dating Goodbye*. On behalf of boyfriends in the late 1990s everywhere, thank you, Josh Harris. Even though I didn't listen to you, you were so right on so many levels.

Looking back I can see how not ready for a relationship I was. Here are the words that come to mind when I think about how I was in that relationship: possessive, jealous, manipulative, emotionally abusive, lustful, depressed. I naively believed that my struggle with lust would have no effect on our relationship. I've never been more wrong. Lust consumed our relationship because of me. I never told a soul until after we broke up.

This is still one of the greatest regrets of my life, not

because it's beyond the forgiveness and redemption of the cross, but because my pride and shame kept me from talking to anyone about it, from telling anyone the truth. Lust kills love because it keeps the truth behind bars.

We broke up during spring break of her senior year in high school, my sophomore year of college. I was devastated. And desperate. When I say desperate, I mean I spent hundreds of dollars buying her a new dress, some new shoes, and her favorite flowers, trying to charm my way back into being her boyfriend. She was done though. Rightly so. Me? Not until I wrote one last letter containing many emo lyrics from many emo bands that I would be embarrassed for you to know I was into.

For the first time since my parents' breakup, I got extremely depressed. The kind of depressed where your bed becomes your best friend. The kind of depressed where you're like the saddest vampire to ever exist because when you come out at night, it's only to play video games. I went to see a counselor. He told me what I had experienced was commonly known as "puppy love." I wanted to murder him. What I felt was exactly the opposite of how seeing a puppy makes you feel.

The Puritans used to say that all growth in the Christian life is downward growth. They did not mean that you are actually getting worse, although it might feel like it. What they meant is that you are slowly beginning to realize that you are worse than you thought, or still think. The Scottish missionary Robert Murray McCheyne wrote in his journal, "The seeds of all sins are in my heart."[4] Given enough soil and water, things I never thought possible can grow from my heart into my life.

This can lead us two places, despair or the cross. Thankfully in my story God drew me closer to the cross. He showed me that I needed Jesus more than I thought I did. This made me love Jesus more than I used to love him. As my understanding of my sin became bigger, so did my understanding of my need for a savior. The cross suddenly became sweeter.

In C. S. Lewis's *Prince Caspian*, Lucy, who has been looking for Aslan, finally finds him.

> "Aslan," said Lucy, "you're bigger."
>> "That is because you are older, little one," answered he.
>> "Not because you are?"
>> "I am not. But every year you grow, you will find me bigger."[5]

So it is in the Christian life. Every year we grow, we will find him bigger.

10:05 a.m., Thursday, November 13,
at Immaculate Consumption

FEELING THE PRESSURE TO GET THE BOOK DONE. I thought I was 75 percent done. Turns out I'm barely over 50 percent. Ugh. In the words of the 90's rap group Geto Boys, my mind's playing tricks on me. The voice in my head is saying, *Write. Write!* and another voice is saying, *You can't. You can't!* Who said that the best feeling isn't writing but having written?

Because I would like to buy that person a cortado while we don't write.

For my wife's thirtieth birthday I got her one gift: a book on being a mom by TV personality Kate Gosselin from the show *Jon & Kate Plus 8*. Nothing says "let me celebrate you as the wonderful and incredible person that you are" like an autobiography of a TLC network reality star. In my defense, she told me she wanted the book. Not in my defense, for my thirtieth birthday she got me a new iPad.

My wife is one of the best gift-givers I know. She loves to surprise loved ones with the things they love. Put in terms of love languages, her leading ones would be acts of service, quality time, and gift giving. Mine are words of affirmation and physical touch. Going to Home Depot on a date to buy an appliance that I would then load and unload without her asking is the romantic whisper of her love language. Mine is her holding me and telling me this book is good.

One of the hardest parts of marriage is the ways in which we constantly miss each other. Instead of living together as affectionate allies, we coexist as distant enemies, like Florida and every other state. Phrases like "I'm sorry" and "please forgive me" and "it was my fault" rarely spill from our lips because they've dried up in our embittered hearts. Instead of moving toward each other in intimacy, we lock the doors of our hearts and can't remember where we put the key.

It's easier to give up on a marriage than it is to give up old habits. The unspoken expectations of family culture, and the unseen attitudes that practically make up our daily lives, create a relational stew that even the hungriest wouldn't touch. Nicolas Sparks's novels, rather than the Bible, shape our view of marriage, which even a Sunday school amount of knowledge tells us is harder than we expect.

What if marriage is supposed to be hard? What if it is supposed to bring out the worst in us? What if marriage is less like going to Target, and more like running a marathon? Soiling your pants in Target? Not a great idea. Soiling your pants in a marathon? Part of the deal. Soiling your pants in marriage? Great dinner party story.

As noted earlier, the longer I'm in ministry the less I believe in premarital counseling. I genuinely believe that it is important, especially the part about telling couples that marriage is harder than they think. And it's also good for helping couples to get on the same page about family, communication, sex, and money. Actually, I'll settle for getting them on the same planet.

The problem is that no one listens during premarital counseling. It's like describing space to a golden retriever. They will smile at you, nod their head a little, and maybe even shake your hand. But they have no idea what you're talking about because they've never been to space. Unless they were one of the puppies in the Disney movie *Space Buddies*. Even then, still no.

So as much as I say, "Listen, wedding sex is typically painful and disappointing," they smile and maybe chuckle a little. Then they text me that night because honeymoon sex was not exactly like any movie or TV show they have ever seen ever in their entire life, ever. Did I put enough *evers* in there? I think we need more. I'm never more thankful for texting than in those moments.

The more unrealistic and idealistic our notions of marriage are, the harder our marriages will be, and the harder they will fall. No matter how beautiful the bride is in her dress, no matter how dapper the groom is in his tux, at the end of the day, marriage, as pastor Dave Harvey says, is two sinners who say "I do."[6] Marriage consists of two people so flawed it will take a lifetime for them to know just how flawed they are and why.

Sometimes I wonder how it is that you could be married to someone for more than ten years and still feel like strangers? There is a peculiar loneliness in marriage. Here is this person who knows more about you than anyone else, yet it feels like they don't really know you at all. Sometimes the person you miss the most is lying right next to you in bed. French philosopher Blaise Pascal wrote, "What a long way it is between knowing God and loving him!"[7] So it is in marriage.

It's funny. My wife knows how I like to squeeze the toothpaste. She knows that I'm not afraid to take two baths in one day. She knows that an expiration date on a bottle of mayonnaise is like a dare to me. And she knows that I have an obsession with shoes that rivals Carrie Bradshaw's in *Sex and the City*. She also knows she can build a better fire than I can. So why is it so hard for me to tell her what I'm really thinking? Why can't we simply sit down face-to-face and talk about what's sitting heavy on our hearts? Why does this person I lay my head next to every night feel more like a ship passing in the night than the anchor of my soul?

A scene in Robert Louis Stevenson's *The Strange Case of Dr. Jekyll and Mr. Hyde* comes to mind when I think about marriage. Dr. Jekyll has transformed into the monstrous Mr. Hyde, and he's locked himself in his laboratory. There's a problem: he's out of the potion that changes him back. Jekyll realizes he will be Hyde forever unless he lets his servants in the room with his potion. He's faced with a choice: let them in to see all his ugliness, or don't let them in and spend the rest of his days alone as Hyde.

Marriage can be like this. It's easier to hide than to let our spouses see the ugliness. It's easier to live alone than to let them behind the door to see the truth about ourselves. Irish playwright Oscar Wilde wrote, "Man is least himself when he talks in his own person. Give him a mask and he will tell you the truth."[8]

Intimacy feels too risky and too hard all at once. The risk is being known and not loved. The hard work is knowing and loving. Even thinking about it makes me want to quit work for the day, pick up a dozen hot Krispy Kremes, and rewatch *Friday Night Lights*. The fact that I can't do this without a spouse judging me is why marriage is both hard and good.

It's been said that God intended marriage more for our holiness than for our happiness, not that the two are mutually exclusive. Happiness and holiness are two sides of the same coin. Who is holier than God? Who is happier than God? The two go together: happiness constraining and informing our view of holiness, holiness constraining and informing our view of happiness. Like Adam and Eve before they tasted forbidden fruit.

If I could talk to high-school-me, I would tell high-school-me a few things now-me has learned about relationships. The first would be this: soul mates are like unicorns. They're incredible, but they don't exist. I don't mean that you never find and marry someone who is perfect for you. You can. You do.

What I mean is that no one person can ever entirely complete you. I remember secretly dreaming about meeting that person who would complete me. And we would share a moment in an elevator with a deaf couple who signs to each other, "You complete me." My ego would drive me to desperate measures in my career, almost destroying our relationship, but then I would go to her sister's house, tell her she completes me, and win her back.

If this sounds like the plot to classic 90's romantic-comedy *Jerry Maguire*, that's because it is. Basically I wanted my love life to be like Jerry Maguire's. I was waiting for the one, my soul mate. And I was going to fail, because it was never going to work.

This is not cynicism. This is me being biblical. There isn't a single person alive, including my spouse, who can bear the weight of my identity.[9] Only God can do that. My life begins with him and ends with him. He has loved me well to give me a wife whose love mirrors his on the best days. Mine too. But that's the thing about mirrors. They don't produce reality; they reflect it.

One of my favorite parts of the University of South Carolina's campus sits right in front of the Thomas Cooper Library, a pond surrounded by brick and benches set in the shade of old oak trees. Students go there to study, talk, or take a nap. I've done all three. The pond is technically called a reflection pool, because its purpose is singular: to reflect the glory that is the old library, whose image is ever upon the surface of the waters.

Marriage is like that. The apostle Paul wrote that marriage is a picture of the kind of love Christ has for his people (Eph. 5). Marriage is a mirror of the reality of God's for-better-or-for-worse love for his people. Reality's bad news is that you never marry your soul mate. The good news is you already have one in Jesus. If a soul mate is someone who perfectly understands you and loves you at all times, then who could ever be that but Jesus?

Knowing this moves us from looking for a soul mate to looking for what Gary Thomas calls a "sole" mate.[10] Not the one who perfectly completes us, but someone who walks along side us as we follow Jesus. Not the only one who makes us happy, but someone to whom, though we sometimes frustrate each other, we have made promises to love to the end.

This view of marriage would bankrupt Disney. I want to write a book called *Realistic Disney*. One chapter would be called "The Little Mermaid Four Years Later." Ariel is bitter that Eric made her move away from the sea to a town in the Midwest. Eric is frustrated that he can't relate to Ariel's friends, mainly because they are all sea creatures.

Another chapter would be "Beauty and the Beast Go to Counseling." Beast wants to do No Shave November with his friends. Belle passive-aggressively withholds sex until he shaves. Their counselor gives them both copies of the book *Boundaries*, which Lumière (the man who was turned into a candelabra) almost burns out of old habit.

The irony is that love is better than romance because real love costs, even demands, a commitment that romance never requires. Everyone cherishes the moment when the bride and groom kiss at their wedding. But no one thinks of the hundreds of moments afterward when those same lips have choices before them. Choices to encourage or complain or shut down or talk or speak words of life or bring up the past in hurtful ways.

But this is where marriage is lived. Joy and sorrow. Sickness and health. Thankfully this is where God lives too.

Chapter Seven

WHERE FRIENDSHIP IS BORN

10:07 a.m., Friday, November 14, at Starbucks

I'M FEELING PARALYZED ABOUT WRITING RIGHT NOW. Not sure why. I feel like everything I'm typing turns to cubic zirconium. It's just trying too hard, trying to be something it's not. The old inner critic is getting after it pretty good too. I need to hire an inner assassin to take care of the situation. Or at least an inner annoying friend to go over there and occupy him for a few hours, overstay his welcome just to shut up the inner critic. Even better, arrange a visit from his inner mom. That way he stays in that state somewhere between confusion and vague anger. This is where good writing music might help. But what do you listen to while writing? Explosions in the Sky's music just makes me want to stop writing and go watch *Friday Night Lights*. Girl Talk worked one time, but it was because I was manic with a deadline. I need an approved list of writing-friendly bands. Better yet, a band that exists entirely to help writers write. Also can we talk about how uncomfortable it is to say you are a writer? Still not there yet. "Author" feels even worse. I'm going with "guy who types stuff then shares it like a middle-schooler moving in for his first kiss."

My new friend and I had just sat down to coffee when I let something slip out that would make us friends forever. It was one of those rare "Me too!" moments that every true friendship seems to have. But this time it wasn't, *"Rushmore* is your favorite Wes Anderson film? Mine too!" It was something else. It was, "You are part of a recovery group? Me too!"

Weakness seems like a weird reason to become friends with someone, unless you were sorted into the Hufflepuff house at Hogwarts. Then it just comes naturally, I guess. But when it comes to doing friendship, we're all way more Hufflepuff than Gryffendor. Friendship is awkward. The best friends are the ones who can handle our awkward.

Imagine yourself as an iceberg for a moment. The tip of the iceberg is what people can see about you. Let's call it your appearance: the kind of clothes you prefer, the way you like to style your hair (or not style it, if you're an engineer), your taste in shoes. Some of us put a lot of thought into our appearance; others of us don't. Either way our appearance is the first impression someone has of us. And if we're honest, sometimes it's the way we choose friends.

Take one stroll through a college campus, and you'll

notice how true this is. Take it again wearing a fanny pack, white New Balance shoes, and some unironic acid-wash jeans, and you'll really notice how true it is. Although if that stroll is by the engineering building, then friendship jackpot!

A little farther down the iceberg is a slightly deeper part of yourself. We can simply call it your experience. What town did you grow up in? What kind of school did you go to? Were your parents upper, middle, or lower class? Where did you typically go on vacation? Another way we choose friends and connect is based upon shared experiences. During my freshman year of college I gravitated toward other freshmen who went to small private schools. We got each other. Especially when it came to effortlessly spending our parents' money at Sam's Club.

Keep going farther beneath the surface, and you reach the deepest part of you. The Bible calls it your heart, the inward reality of yourself. Who you really are. What you really love. What you're like behind closed doors. What drives you. What enslaves you. As author-professor Brené Brown says, you are your secrets.[1]

This part is the hardest to share, yet this is the part we live with, and in, the most. This is the part we're glad is beneath the surface so no one can see it. The problem is sometimes reality bumps up against it, and the *Titanic* that is the appearance you desperately want to keep up begins to sink. (My goal was to work at least one *Titanic* reference into this book. Mission accomplished.)

Just before writing this, I grabbed coffee with a friend

and old college roommate. We grew up together. Went to the same school all our lives. Even went to the same preschool. We both loved basketball. In our day we were obsessed with the same bands and are still a little ashamed to admit how many of their concerts we went to. We ended up living together in college. It wasn't until we recently reconnected, though, that we realized how little about each other's hearts we really knew. Everything we knew about each other was simply the tip of the iceberg. There was an entire massive surface underneath the water we had no idea about.

The apostle Paul wrote about this in his own way in Philippians 3, where he gives his resume. For a large part of his life, he led with his strengths—his family, his religious and academic pedigree, his impressive credentials as a religious leader in the community. All the reasons people should be impressed by him. You get the feeling Paul had a lot of drop-the-mic moments in his heart, moments when he wanted others to stand in awe of him.

Then something crazy happened. He met Jesus, and his entire life was flipped upside down. What was once impressive to him now paled in comparison to the impression Jesus made upon him, the joy of knowing him, the worth of being found in him. And what he once thought was impressive about himself, his resume, began to be a source of shame. He had sought many good things, but he had sought them for proud and selfish reasons.

Paul went on to say in 2 Corinthians that this whole experience caused him to lead with his weaknesses. It's not that he didn't have strengths. He did. Lots of them. But in terms of what he wanted people to know about him most, he led with the reasons he didn't have it all together, the reasons he needed grace and was lost without it. He now was leading with vulnerability instead of admirability. This is the radical thing about the way Paul did relationship.

Friendship is born in the moments the iceberg gets flipped over, where what's beneath the surface emerges, when our hearts are opened up and revealed. Some of us are lonely, but it's not for lack of people who dress like us and talk like us and live like us and vacation like us. Some of us are lonely because the friends we have are tip-of-the-iceberg friends. We never venture to go beneath the surface because it's cold and we're scared. (Where is Leonard DiCaprio when you need him?)

One of the ways we can get beneath the surface in each other's lives involves what my friend Jon Acuff calls the "gift of going second."[2] It is those moments where we dare to take what's inside and bring it out of ourselves. Maybe it's sharing about something that has been a struggle for years. Or maybe it's saying something out loud that has been rolling around in your heart like a hamster in one of those clear balls. When you say it first or share it first, you're giving the gift of going second, creating a sacred space in which we can know and accept each other as we really are, not as we pretend to be. This is the best kind of present. Especially if it's at Christmas and comes complete with one of those huge tins of three kinds of popcorn. If it comes with fruitcake, run.

The danger is that friends are like vampires: you invite

them in and hope they don't suck the life right out of you. That possibility is typically why we're afraid to invite people in. We've all been burned in friendship. Some of us have made promises to never let anyone in ever again. Trusting another human being is simple, but it's not easy. Driven by the fear that we will be relationally sifted and found wanting, we shrink from friendship, like a vampire shrinking from the sun.

The hard work of friendship is entrusting your heart to another and risking your story while at the same time holding your friend's story carefully. Friends cannot hold the weight of your identity, but you should be able to trust them with the weight of your story—your dreams and fears, your desires and struggles, the things that make you yourself, past and present. This is the hard work of friendship, the art of friendship.

Basketball star Kobe Bryant recently opened up about friendship in an interview with Chuck Klosterman in *GQ* magazine, and what he said was painfully honest: "I have good relationships with players around the league. . . . But in terms of having one of those great, bonding friendships— that's something I will probably never have. And it's not some smug thing. It's a weakness. It's a weakness."[3]

Echoing from his words are both the longing and the fear of deep friendship. But friends are not like gravy; they are meat and potatoes. We need them. The sad reality is most of us are like Kobe: we see friends as optional because they might get in the way of what we want.

A counselor told me that in all your relationships you're

always doing one of two things: ministry or manipulation. I'm always either serving you for God's purposes or using you for my own. The problem is that manipulation feels a lot safer. It keeps me in the position of control without ever putting me in the position of need. Ministry, on the other hand, is a constant sacrificing of self for the love of others. It's not shrinking back from one another in indifference, but moving toward one another in bold love. And love always puts you in a vulnerable position.

Think about David and Jonathan's friendship in 1 Samuel. The moment that forever sealed them as true friends happened when David was on the run from Jonathan's father, Saul. Jonathan was the rightful heir to the throne, yet David stood as the greatest threat to the throne there was. Saul had David on the ropes, ready to snuff out the threat. Saul was all manipulation. He would have made a great *Game of Thrones* character.

And Jonathan? He did something radically different. Instead of beheading David when he had the chance, he gave him his armor and his shield. Instead of putting David in his place, he put himself in David's place, the place of vulnerability, weakness, and potential defeat. He made himself literally vulnerable to David. And their friendship was forever cemented. Jonathan was all ministry.

Ministry is vulnerability. I don't mean that you're always oversharing, or that you're sharing in ways that try to manipulate people into liking or respecting you. What I mean by "ministering" is faithfully putting yourself in a position where you could be hurt or, worse, rejected. It's been said that a friend is a gift you give yourself. Maybe it's better to say friendship is giving someone the gift of yourself. You in all your ruined glory, waiting to be opened and enjoyed. The present of your presence. That's the gift we need.

This is exactly what manipulation seeks to avoid. You're always unwrapping the presents of others, but never giving yourself, never letting yourself be opened and enjoyed. Because what if someone unwraps you and he's disappointed? Or what if someone opens you and decides to take you to Walmart and exchange you for something better? Manipulation is a way of avoiding the risk of love. I've seen *Toy Story*. I know how this works.

Tim Keller said, "Real friends always let you in, and they never let you down."[4] Friends want you to know them, but they also want to love you. They aren't afraid of you loving them, but neither are they afraid of knowing you. Friendship is a constant combination of jabbing with being known, and hooking with being loved. (You can probably tell from that metaphor that I've never actually boxed.)

This means friendship has two common enemies: fakeness and flakiness. Both are ways of avoiding vulnerability. Both are ways of not having to trust people. Both are ways of operating out of the fear that no one could actually know you and love you. This feels like the *Sophie's Choice* of every relationship: known or loved, but not both.

There's a scene in the movie *Babe* that always makes me cry. It's when the farm animals tell Babe, the charming pig training as a prize-winning sheepdog, that no matter if he wins the prize at the State Fair, he's going to be turned into ham for Thanksgiving dinner. Babe doesn't take this news well and runs away. He gets lost in a storm and almost dies. Thankfully Farmer Hoggett goes looking for him, finds him, and brings him home. Farmer Hoggett begins nursing Babe back to health. Then he does something incredibly strange. He begins singing to him, even dancing for him. The other farm animals are so shocked that they crowd their faces into the windows of the house to watch, because what kind of a farmer sings and dances over a pig?

What kind of a God sings over sinners and delights in them? He knows us at our worst yet loves us at his best. I've always loved the way theologian J. I. Packer put it:

> This is momentous knowledge. There is unspeakable comfort—the sort of comfort that energizes, be it said, not enervates—in knowing that God is constantly taking knowledge of me in love and watching over me for my good. There is tremendous relief in knowing that his love to me is utterly realistic, based at every point on prior knowledge of the worst about me, so that no discovery now can disillusion him about me, in the way I am so often disillusioned about myself, and quench his determination to bless me.[5]

If vulnerability is where friendship is born, then being known and loved by the Friend of Sinners is where vulnerability is born. Jonathan gave up the potential of the throne for David, but Jesus left his throne for us. Jonathan gave up his armor for David, but Jesus gave up his life for us. He's the only friend who fully lets us in and never lets us down. All other friends will fail, but he remains faithful. Jesus is the True and Better Samwise Gamgee,[6] there for us to Mordor and back, loving us in ways we don't even realize we need.

The courage to let others in is found in the arms of a God who has let us all the way in. We are so far in that he calls us his sons and daughters. We are so far in that we can never be out. We are so far in that there is no need to RSVP to the housewarming party for the new heavens and new earth because the party won't happen without us.

The strength not to let others down is found in a God who will never let us down. His presence for us isn't an empty promise. It's the hidden reality of the universe, the one that keeps it going. God's faithfulness isn't the cross-stitching on your grandmother's pillow. It's the reality that made the fabric for the pillow possible in the first place. And it's still the best place to lay your head at night.

As Chris Rock said, when you meet someone for the first time you don't meet them; you meet their representative.[7] It's funny, but there's a way we do this even with God, maybe especially with God. The way to begin bringing yourself to that first meeting is to be befriended by a God who meets you where you are, not where you should be, who loves you as you are, not as you should be. That kind of friendship changes the kind of friends we are.

10:25 a.m., Monday, November 17, at
McDonald's. That's right. McDonald's.

I HAVEN'T EATEN AT A MCDONALD'S IN WELL OVER A year, and, boy, does it feel good to be home. It's like the high school sweetheart you avoid because getting back in touch with her might end your marriage. Or in McDonald's case, your life. Tell me what tastes better than McDonald's? McDonald's food is like wanting to meet Aslan in Narnia: it's not real, but you wish it were. Or maybe it's more like meeting Voldemort at Hogwarts, because it's amazingly powerful and it will kill you.

One of the first jokes I ever attempted on Twitter was this: "If Hide and Seek were a game where you hid your true feelings and sought approval from everyone, then I'm winning." Not a great joke, but it does capture the way I do friendship. I hide what I really feel and think while I seek out what you feel and think, and then I will make sure the thoughts and feelings I share with you match yours. I act like a chameleon, one who can talk and has opinions strikingly similar to yours.

The reality is we all hide from each other, and as I mentioned earlier, we all want to be found. A friend is someone who is looking for us, who wants to find us. That's what friendship is: a commitment to finding each other and being found.

The trouble with being found is that it means you've been lost. And admitting you're lost is a blow to your pride, especially when you're admitting things related to marriage or work or parenting or addictions. There's a way of being lost inside that even though you're desperate for someone to find you, you're more desperate to hide that "lostness" and keep it from crying too loudly for help. The hand of pride muffles the mouth of vulnerability.

My favorite scene in *Lés Miserables* is when Jean Valjean

gets word that Javert has found a man who Javert thinks is Valjean and is about to lock him away. Valjean begins an intense dialogue with himself about what he should do. Does he reveal himself to the courts, or does he keep the new life and new name he's been peacefully building for years? He's not sure if he should reveal himself, because revealing himself will be painful. But he decides he must. So he unbuttons his shirt and reveals his prison number, which he then declares to the court, "24601." He reveals the most shameful thing about him in order to bring life to another.

Valjean's tattoo is the one I've always wanted, and I haven't gotten it for two reasons. One, it feels maybe a little cliché, like getting "Timshel"[8] on your inner arm because you love not John Steinbeck's *East of Eden* but Mumford & Sons. (In the bathroom of a really hipster bar, I noticed where someone had taken a Sharpie marker and written "Tishmel," and it's still one of my favorite things ever. Now that would make a great tattoo.) The second reason is I don't have the body for it. More on this in a later chapter.

Tattoo or not, "24601 friends" are the kind of friends we need and the kind of friends we need to be. They are friends who aren't afraid to let you know they have a past, that they've messed up, that they don't have it all together. Because to admit you have a past is to also admit that you have a present. Not that your past defines you. It doesn't. But it most definitely shapes you. The ways we've been sinned against always shape the ways we sin. "24601 friends" are those who aren't afraid to confess sin and help bear the burdens of the ways we've been sinned against.

One of my favorite nights in recent years happened with a group of friends I get together with every Tuesday night. This particular night we decided to build a fire in a fire pit in my backyard. Something about fires draws out conversation from guys. Probably because you can talk while looking at the fire instead of at each other. Fires are a conversational gift to guys.

As we sat around that fire, we shared our stories of abuse—sexual abuse, to be specific. Sadly most of us had a story. It was a weird night. It was also one of the most encouraging nights of my life. Not because hearing my friends' stories wasn't hard, but because I wasn't alone. Because I have "24601 friends" who aren't afraid to let me know who they really are and who aren't afraid to know who I really am. "24601 friends" don't shrink from the truth, the sad, hard, sometimes devastating truth. "24601 friends" want you to be found. And they're not afraid of what they might find.

I don't mean to make finding true friends sound easy. It's not. There's a little bit of mystery, I think, to how two people's souls get knitted together in lasting friendship. There have been times in my life when I felt I had these kinds of friends. There have been other seasons when I didn't and felt lonely. There have been still other seasons when what was a good friendship crashed upon the rocks of conflict and betrayal. Finding and keeping dear friends is hard.

This was what made *I Love You, Man* such an endearing film. Paul Rudd gets engaged, and as his fiancée begins calling all her friends, it suddenly dawns on both of them that he doesn't really have any friends. He has coworkers and acquaintances. But when it comes to friendship, he's a bit of a loner. He realizes it's a problem. He also realizes you don't just suddenly become best friends with someone. What do you do when you realize you don't have any real friends?

The last thing you do is go get friends for the sake of having friends. No amount of Twitter followers or Facebook friends can ever make up for real-life friends who actually like you. This is also why there isn't a dating app like Tinder for friendship. Friends have to actually have something in common beyond their appearances. As C. S. Lewis noted:

> The very condition of having Friends is that we should want something else besides Friends. Where the truthful answer to the question "Do you see the same truth?" would be "I see nothing and I don't care about the truth; I only want a Friend," no Friendship can arise—though Affection of course may. There would be nothing for the Friendship to be about; and Friendship must be about something, even if it were only an enthusiasm for dominoes or white mice. Those who have nothing can share nothing; those who are going nowhere can have no fellow-travelers.[9]

Friendship is the relational dance of moving back and forth between face-to-face and side-by-side love. Face-to-face love seeks to look into your soul and know you through and through. Side-by-side love seeks to join you as you walk through life together. We need the embrace of both kinds of love. The one that isn't afraid to hold our face, and the other that isn't afraid to put its arm around our shoulders.

It's typically true, too, that we're better at one form of love than the other. One of the most startling realizations my wife and I have had in marriage counseling occurred when we went over our Myers-Briggs personality test results. Our counselor told us that 80 percent of men were thinkers, and 80 percent of women were feelers. The problem is my wife is a thinker and I am a feeler. We're both in the relational minority when it comes to our gender's preference in the way we spend time together. I want to sit down over coffee and talk about how you're feeling about what you're feeling. My wife, a strikingly beautiful woman, would rather go build something.

Most guys typically don't want to sit down for coffee and talk about their feelings. Most women typically don't want to go build something while they avoid talking about their feelings. This means, for my wife and me, finding friends has in some ways been a lifelong struggle. We have incredible friends, but it's hard for us to make friends in the typical way.

What we've learned over the years is that we both need to grow in the way we do friendship. I need to grow in my ability and desire to do side-by-side love. She needs to grow in her ability and desire to do face-to-face love. Maybe every Christmas I should just give her a gift card for counseling, and she should just give me a gift card for Home Depot, and we could shame each other into changing.

Now, who wants to go grab some Starbucks and talk about their most painful memory from middle school and how it shapes you today?

Chapter Eight

CALLING ALL INTROVERTS
(They Probably Won't Pick Up)

1:27 p.m., Monday, November 17, at home

I'M WRITING IN SWEATPANTS IN THE MIDDLE OF THE afternoon. Maybe this whole writing thing isn't so bad after all. Although sweatpants are kind of like the cereal of clothes. They're amazing pretty much any time of day. Also they make you feel a little lazy. A lot lazy. Sweatpants shouldn't come with "Juicy" written on the back of them. They should come with "Listen, it's been a long week" written on the back instead. Either way I've found my favorite writing clothes. Now if only there were a way I could wear them in public and still be married.

Several years ago I took a group of college students to Chicago to work with a ministry on the South Side. There were other groups there as well, easily one hundred of us in

127

all. We were staying the week, helping in schools and after-school programs, as well as lending some extra hands to various construction projects in the neighborhood. As we were settling in, claiming corners and blowing up air mattresses, I reached into my bag and pulled back in horror. Here I was about to spend a week with one hundred people, ninety of them strangers, and I had forgotten my headphones.

Headphones are to an introvert what the cloak of invisibility is to Harry Potter. Slipping them on is a way of becoming invisible. The bigger the headphones, the better. As a rule I'm against ear buds. The message they send is ambiguous: "I'm sort of listening to something, but you can still talk to me." Give me headphones big enough for Dumbo, cans that say, "Don't you dare try to talk to me right now." You can tell how big an introvert someone is by how big their headphones are. At least you should be able to.

For most of my life I've been the quiet, reserved type who has a hard time looking people in the eyes. I've always been suspicious of people who get a little too excited about something. Let's call them extroverts. By the way, I'm on my fourth cup of coffee for the day. Is this what being an extrovert feels like all the time?

When it comes to small talk, I make toddlers look like social geniuses. Remember that Jodie Foster movie *Nell*? If you've seen that, then you've seen me at a party. Better yet, if you've seen me looking at my phone, then you've seen me at a party. No matter what scientists say, if you've seen an introvert at a party, you've seen a ghost. Introverts don't get ready for a party; they gather strength for a party.

Thankfully we live in a day that is made for intro-verts. Headphones abound. Self-checkout lines have been invented. It's socially acceptable to look at your phone instead of talking to people. Can you imagine being an introvert in the 1800s? Bathrooms couldn't double as panic rooms because they were outhouses that required you to leave the comfort of the indoors, and even your horse tried to look you in the eyes.

I've felt a lot of shame in my life for being quiet and reserved. Why can't I look people in the eyes? Why is it so hard for me to make small talk at a party? Why does being around people make me feel tired? Why does being alone help me feel recharged? Why isn't it socially acceptable for me to go to a movie by myself and enjoy it more than if I were with a group of friends? Why do I hate myself when someone catches me going to a movie by myself and feel the need to pretend to be waiting for a friend in the bathroom or catching up with a friend outside? I've done both.

This is the part of the book where I want to say up front that I realize a lot of this might sound like psycho-babble. I'm not sure what you make of personality tests, or if you have your Myers-Briggs letters[1] tattooed across your knuckles (my second favorite tattoo idea). I'll lay my cards on the table and say that I find personality tests helpful in understanding a person, but unhelpful in defining them as a person. You are more than your Myers-Briggs type. That doesn't mean it might not be helpful in understanding yourself more.

The tension for me was the tension John Calvin said

was the foundation of all theology: knowledge of God and knowledge of self.[2] Neither cancels out the other, but instead each enhances the other. Knowledge of God leads to knowledge of self, and vice versa. This doesn't mean we spend our lives trying to figure out Jesus' personality type. It means we see the glory of God displayed in all kinds of personality types. One of the most glorious things about God is his love for variety and diversity. It's one of the ways the world sings his praises, whether it knows it or not.

The trouble comes when I use my personality type as an excuse not to love others well. Introverts still have to go to a friend's birthday party and make a decent toast. Extroverts still have to grab coffee with a friend and not dominate the conversation but actually listen. Being an introvert isn't a get-out-of-jail-free card for talking to people. Being an extrovert isn't a pass-go card for listening to others' problems. And if you actually like Monopoly and are tracking with that analogy, you're probably an introvert. This is coming from someone who was designated Tami Taylor in a *Friday Night Lights* personality quiz, so you know you can trust what I say.

One of the most comforting things to me about the Bible is that its writers and its characters all had incredibly varied personalities. Moses was afraid to speak in public, yet it seemed hard for Peter to know when to shut up. Jonah kind of hated people, yet Paul seemed to genuinely love people of all kinds. By the way, as an introvert, I've always been drawn to Jonah: being inside a whale sounds gross but also kind of incredible in terms of alone time. Martha seemed to be a "do-er," while her sister Mary was more of a "be-er." The reality is God loves and uses all kinds of people with all kinds of personalities. He even seems to use their flaws for his purposes, which for an introvert who hates public speaking yet preaches every week is incredibly comforting.

It's trendy these days to talk about personality types. We do it all the time on Facebook. Which *New Girl* Character Are You? Which State Should You Really Live In? I'm still waiting for Which Starburst Flavor Are You? Yellow. The answer is we are all Yellow.

Or think about the different houses in *Harry Potter,* the different districts in *The Hunger Games,* or the different factions in *Divergent.* Each is broken down according to personality, disposition, and aptitude. Which house would you be sorted into? Which district would you live in? Which faction would you test into?

In fact, thinking about your personality type seems to be a tool for finding your way in the world, for knowing your strengths and weaknesses. It's hard to follow, much less be sure of, your life's calling if you're unsure of what your gifts are and what they're not. Theologian Frederick Buechner wrote, "The place God calls you to is the place where your deep gladness and the world's deep hunger meet."[3] Understanding your personality is another way of understanding where your deep gladness might intersect with the world's deep hunger.

Since we long to know our place in the world, we long to know ourselves first. This is a long process we never quite get to the end of, though we make progress and have moments of revelation. Thankfully who we thought we'd be at age twenty-three is different from who we actually are at age thirty-three. When I was twenty-three, I seriously contemplated being both a landscaper and a hairdresser. I had conversations with different employers about both. The hairdresser wasn't hiring, and the landscaper was honest and told me, "You're a hard worker, but I don't think you were meant to run a crew." I wanted to work with my hands. It seems, at least for now, that God wants me to work with words. As Susan Cain said, "Everyone shines, given the right lighting. For some, it's a Broadway spotlight, for others, a lamplit desk."[4]

Years ago I read a book by Adam McHugh called *Introverts in the Church*. I had never read a Christian leader talking about what it means to lead as an introvert. Like any good introvert, I sheepishly began recommending the book to all my friends, because if there is one thing introverts are good at, it's recommending books.

One line in particular has stayed with me. "Becoming a Christian is not tantamount [to] becoming an extrovert."[5] We could also add that being a Christian is not tantamount to being an extrovert, yet a casual visit to almost any Christian gathering could lead you to conclude the opposite. This varies from group to group, but the pressure is there. Typically this is because we've exalted a method (or methods) over the message.

If you reduce evangelism, for example, to a narrow range of actions that require cold turkey boldness mixed with warm, pithy, and persuasive conversational skills, then only extroverts could ever do it. On the other hand, if you broaden evangelism to include both the creative arts, as well as deep one-on-one conversations over coffee or tea, then introverts are indispensable. Eugene Peterson, pastor and author, likes to ask not how many people have you talked to about Christ this week, but "how many people have you listened to in Christ this week?"[6]

If you have a method or formula more than you have a message or truth, then you implicitly rule out all the personality types that can't pull off your method or formula. If you have a message, however, then you invite all kinds of personality types to embody and reflect that message through a variety of different gifts and methods. This is exactly what Paul was getting at in 1 Corinthians when he compared the church to a body, with different members being like different parts of the body, all working together with none being more important than the other. How beautiful are the feet that bring good news, Isaiah tells us. But where would the mouth be if the feet couldn't take it to places where it might be heard? Where would the feet be if the brain couldn't tell them how and where to walk?

I remember sitting down in Starbucks with a student and talking about McHugh's book. We both had our Chai tea lattes and were sipping them quietly, probably looking down a lot. She was feeling shame for getting nervous about talking to people before and after campus meetings. Her roommate was an extreme extrovert, the kind that makes people who sip Chai tea lattes in Starbucks a little nervous. She was friendly and enthusiastic, and people loved to be around her, and my friend was equal parts jealous and insecure. Why couldn't she just be more like her roommate? That was the question she was asking through tears. (If I had a dollar for how many times I've cried or been with someone who cried in Starbucks, I might be able to afford a venti next time.)

This is the hard thing about personalities. A lot of us genuinely believe something is wrong with us because we don't have the personality we think we want—a more talkative one, a more charming one, a more organized one, a more attractive one. Most of us feel like we have a disastrous personality. Unless you're an ENTJ. Then you're pretty sure everyone has a disastrous personality except you, and you have a plan to fix that. (That was another Myers-Briggs joke. I really should get some kind of referral fee.)

The beautiful thing about the gospel is that it's personality blind. Maybe it's better to say that it speaks to every personality. It tells Type A people to come and find rest for their weary, workaholic souls. It tells Type B people that there is a kingdom of grace and renewal worth working and giving their lives for. It tells the strong to be weak, and the weak to be strong. It tells the loud to listen, and the quiet to speak.

The gospel is also best spoken when every personality speaks it in its own way. That means there are certain personalities only you can reach. It doesn't mean we need to divide into different factions or districts or houses. It simply means that the gospel reflected through your personality is a beautiful thing. And if you and your disastrous personality were to stop reflecting the gospel, there would be a little less beauty in the world. This feels like a time to quote Coach Taylor from *Friday Night Lights*: "Clear eyes. Full hearts. Can't lose."

8:34 a.m., Friday, November 21, in a friend's
empty apartment, which is the best

I GOT DONUTS FOR THE KIDS THIS MORNING BEFORE school. I ate only less than half of one. Who have I become? Donuts are my jam. Especially if they are filled with raspberry jelly. Unfortunately I'm in one of those phases where I've lost weight, but feel like I'm slipping in the habits that helped me get here, and I'm extremely self-conscious about it. Thanksgiving is the worst time of year to be worrying about your weight. It's like worrying about whether you should drink while standing in the checkout line at a liquor store. On the other hand, Thanksgiving is my favorite time of year because it's socially acceptable to talk about all your favorite foods.

On December 13, 2003, I said, "I do" to an extrovert. I had no idea that this would mean the following: her favorite place to be is at a party with old friends and new friends alike. She loves to talk on the phone and wants me not only to love talking on the phone as much as she does, but also to want to call her a lot just to check in and tell her how my day is going. She does not want to lie down on the couch with me and watch Netflix all day.

I'm not sure which she loves more, lists or people. She is not afraid to talk to strangers wherever we are: football games, the grocery store, the kids' school. She enjoys talking to repairmen when they come to fix an appliance, instead of wanting to hide upstairs like me. She loves to ask questions, lots of questions, during movies. Did I mention how much she loves to talk on the phone? I don't mean be on the phone. I mean actually pick up the phone and call other people like it's 1989.

I could write an entire book about how much I don't like talking on the phone. How a character in a horror movie feels when the phone rings is how I always feel when the phone rings. I genuinely believe returning a text with a phone call is one of the worst things you could ever do to someone. It's like saying, "Oh you like French fries? Here is a kale smoothie."

But I'm glad my wife is an extrovert. If she weren't, who would ever call my family back? We would both be fighting over who gets to read for hours in the bath alone, or we would get a babysitter and go see different movies alone and then not tell each other about them. We would never get invited to parties because our friends would be convinced we were using them for our mime school training.

What I'm trying to say is that I'm thankful for people who don't have my personality, because the world would be more black and white, less color, if they did. I'm also thankful for my personality. Not because I think it's great. I don't. I'm an ISFP who also happens to be an Enneagram Type Three, which means I live and die by what others think of me. Actually, I live and die based on what I think others think of me. It's exhausting. But the world needs ISFPs like me.

In *Planes, Trains and Automobiles*, John Candy's character—a quiet, reserved, overall nice guy—gets stuck with Steve Martin, who is having a really, really bad day and is aggressively taking it out on everyone, Candy most of all. There's a scene in the hotel where Martin is going off on Candy, and Candy interrupts him, stands up for himself for the first time in the whole movie, and simply says, "I, I, I like me!" The way he says it sounds like he's just believed it for the first time.

The gospel frees you to like yourself, not because you're so great, but because Jesus loves you. More than that, he likes you. As one of my best friends once asked me, "Do you believe that Jesus doesn't just love you, but that he likes you? You should. He does." Jesus went to the cross because he wants you and your disastrous personality to be present with him for eternity in the new heavens and new earth. He doesn't tolerate you in his love. He enjoys you in his like. The love of Jesus frees you to be okay with yourself.

I'm not sure what your quote was under your senior picture in your high school yearbook, or if you even had one. I remember mine. It was a touch self-righteous C. S. Lewis quote: "God cannot give us a peace and happiness apart from himself because it is not there. There is no such thing."[7]

I also remember another quote in the yearbook, from a guy in our class who was a bit of a loner: "Could I have been anyone other than me?" It's actually a line from Dave Matthews Band's "Dancing Nancies." It still makes me sad to think about how he must have felt all those years we sat near each other in class. I had no idea.

The good news of the gospel is that the Lord answers that question and says, "It's not anyone other than you that I want." The Lord chooses a relationship with us, in the words of Beyoncé, flaws and all. The thing about being chosen is it does not mean you are choice.[8] You don't have it all together. But you do have it all if you have friendship with the God of the universe, because to be chosen means that all your flaws and quirks and weirdness and ugliness could not turn away the love of God.

And the people of God aren't being the people of God unless we're choosing people the way God chooses. Choosing friendship with those not like ourselves. Choosing to love those the world deems weird, odd, or ugly. Choosing relationships with people with all kinds of disastrous character flaws. Dating and marrying people with polar opposite personalities, because we are better and fuller together than we would ever be apart.

The thing that introverts and extroverts have in common isn't that we like all the same things or do everything in the same way. The thing we have in common is that we need each other. If we didn't, who would be there to talk, and who would be there to listen?

Chapter Nine

DONUTS ARE A WHOLE FOOD IF YOU TAKE OUT THE W

12:33 p.m., Friday, November 21, still
at my friend's empty apartment

BEFORE I WRITE, CAN WE TALK ABOUT HOW INCREDIBLE
being in someone else's apartment while they're not there is?
I would be lying if I said I haven't taken a bath already. With
bubbles. Just like John Steinbeck used to do. If there is such
a thing as a writing process, mine definitely includes bubble
baths. Being alone is great. Being alone in a bathtub is a little
taste of heaven. In fact, I hope Jesus' second words to me, after
"Well done, my good and faithful servant," are, "Wait until you
see the bathtub I've got waiting for you."

My freshman year of college I didn't gain the "freshman fifteen." I gained a freshman fifty. I came into college

somewhere around 190 pounds and graduated pushing 250. I was like one of those pythons that eats an entire deer, only I was eating Wendy's and IHOP. I know that weight is like age: it's just a number. A number that, as it gets higher, makes you mouth cuss words to yourself in the mirror and hate yourself just a little bit more.

The weight gain didn't happen overnight. It was a combination of several things: four or more meals a day, plus snacks. Because what feels better than rolling through the Wendy's drive-thru at one thirty in the morning? They should call fast-food drive-thru's "lanes of shame." The loneliest feeling in the world is when you, sitting in your car at a Wendy's drive-thru, accidentally make eye contact through the window with a fellow fast-food traveler enjoying his meal as you slowly pull away.

I also slept a lot. Remember? I was incredibly depressed in college. One time my friends on my hall were so impressed at how late I was sleeping that they set an alarm clock for five in the afternoon, gathered around my door, and applauded as the alarm went off and I opened the door to see what the commotion was. I would sleep entire days away. The down side was I missed a lot of classes. The upside was it's the closest I've ever been to being a bear.

Because of my depression, I was on two different medications, Effexor and Depakote. One was an antidepressant; the other, a mood stabilizer. The good news was they helped me get my head above the dark cloud of my depression. The bad news was it was hard to keep my head there for long because the drugs also caused extreme, rapid weight gain. I felt a kinship with Fat Bastard in the *Austin Powers* movies: "I eat because I'm unhappy. And I'm unhappy because I eat." The only thing worse than feeling depressed is feeling fat and depressed.

Exercise became like a story from George Washington's biography, something you read about in books, but isn't part of your life. Playing sports in high school ensures that exercise is part of your life. In college it's a different story. No one is running sprints during intramural basketball practice.

Weight is a fountain of shame for many of us, especially if like me your weight has fluctuated for most of your life. It's funny what you remember. Having to shop at the husky section at Belk. Never wanting to wear sweaters. A friend of my parents who owned a clothing store laughing and saying, "You must be eating plenty of bowls of cereal." (Three after school most days, to be exact.) My grandmother saying my legs looked like tree trunks. Words are powerful. Words about weight are more powerful than most. So powerful they ring in your ears for a lifetime.

Just this morning I squeezed into a pair of size thirty-four corduroys that are so tight I can practically hear the button screaming. If I could speak button, I'm sure I'd hear something like, "Ahhhh! It hurts! It hurts so bad!" Thankfully I don't speak button. I do, however, realize what I'm doing. I'm in denial that I need to move to a size thirty-six. I can't bear to face this. I worked hard on my weight during the summer, but since then I've joined a gang called Five Guys Burgers and Fries and am slowly undoing my hard work, one double cheeseburger with barbeque sauce at a time. Being a size thirty-four means I can be okay with myself; being a thirty-six, a little less so. Why do I think that my worth is directly tied to my waist size?

I grew up in one of those families that plans everything around food. Holidays, vacations, parties. I love that about my family and about living in the South. I'm not sure if good food is a good excuse for a party, or if a party is a good excuse for good food. I am sure that there is no such thing as a good party without good food. This certainty makes me want to get a Sharpie and change the *G*s to *F*s on those "Life Is Good" shirts.

My belief in this matter has caused some tension in my marriage, especially when it comes to what we do on vacation. We realized this when we got back from our honeymoon and people asked us how it was. My wife said, "So great!" and I said, "It was good but the food was terrible."

I went to a school growing up that hadn't caught wind of the healthy food movement. This was the 1990s, and we didn't have Netflix and a thousand documentaries telling us why fast food is evil. So we ate it. Lots of it. We had a two week rotation: Captain D's, Pizza Hut, Chick-fil-A, a local Chinese restaurant, Burger King, KFC, Taco Bell, a local Italian restaurant, Papa John's, and more Chick-fil-A. Our eating habits were like smoking in the sixties: we didn't know any better, and it was incredible.

Imagine my dismay years later when I watched the documentary *Food Inc.* with my wife. It was like watching my entire childhood crumble to ashes. I'm pretty sure I cried, not so much for the animals and their awful, inhumane conditions, or for the way we put things into our bodies that are so processed they're almost not food. No, I cried because I knew what it meant. I could never again order a number six combo meal from Wendy's, the spicy chicken sandwich with fries (duh), a large sweet tea, and a medium chocolate Frosty, without guilt and hesitation. It was like that moment in a relationship when you know you're going to break up but keep dating anyway, lying to yourself because facing the truth is too painful.

For me food has always been primarily about comfort. Food was always there for me. My parents might be getting divorced, I'd think, but this pizza isn't going anywhere except my stomach. Food became a way of coping with life, in all its sadness and hardness. It's supposed to be used as energy that I then put into life. It's not supposed to be life itself. I know that's how it's meant to be. But that's not how I want it to be. If food is a gift, some of us are hoarders.

In *The Way of Ignorance*, the poet and farmer Wendell Berry talks about how he learned again the importance of farming, of the slowness of pace, and the presence required. He relearned a new way of doing life. He wrote that modernity ushered in "an era of limitlessness, or the illusion thereof, and this in itself is a sort of wonder. My grandfather lived a life of limits, both suffered and strictly observed, in a world of limits. I learned much of that world from him and others, and then I changed; I entered the world of labor-saving machines and of limitless cheap fossil fuel. It would take me years of reading, thought, and experience to learn again that in this world limits are not only inescapable but indispensable."[1]

Approaching food in a life-giving way doesn't mean approaching it without enjoyment or celebration or even feasting. It means approaching food within the limits both in terms of quantity and quality of the body God gives us. Food matters because our bodies matter. Our bodies matter because we matter. We know that we matter because the Son of God himself at this very moment has a body—the very body that we will have, too, in that glorious physical place Scripture calls the new heavens and new earth.

Limits is a word we don't much care for. My wife and I are learning this with our son. He's eight years old and, like his dad, loves to eat. Just yesterday he nearly threw a bowl of ice cream at his grandmother because she told him he couldn't have three huge scoops of ice cream, especially after he just ate an entire cup of yogurt. He got mad about food. He does that a lot, and I find it hard to remember two things. One, he is eight years old, and learning about limits. Two, I am thirty-four years old and still get mad and pout when my wife breaks it to me that we're eating leftovers. I may hide it a little better now than previously, but food still has Sauron-like power over me.

Food has power over a lot of my students too. Some run to it for comfort and, like me, put on the freshman fifteen or twenty or thirty. Others have a relationship with food more defined by control, either by not eating in the name of being the kind of skinny they want to be (typically much skinnier than they ever should be), or by immediately remedying a momentary lapse of eating too much by closing a bathroom door and quietly getting it all out.

In many ways our relationship with food is like our relationship with sex, an incredible gift that seems impossibly hard to receive with grace. Some of us seem to believe that if we could just get enough of the food we want, we would be happy. Others of us seem to believe that if we could just get down to the weight we want, then we'd be content. Both types fail to realize that temporary achievements make for poor saviors. The fridge may be full, but it can't make us full. The scale may read what we want, but it can't give us what we want. Because what we really want isn't our favorite foods or to be a certain weight. What we really want is to know deep down that we're okay.

This is what makes my relationship with food so complicated. I want too much of foods that aren't good for me because I don't feel okay. I want to lose twenty more pounds because I think then I'll finally be okay. What I'm really craving is someone who will tell me that I am okay. Because most of the time I don't feel okay.

2:34 p.m., Tuesday, December 2, at Starbucks

NOTHING LIKE WRITING AFTER AN AWKWARD ENCOUNter with a barista. You would think talking to baristas would come naturally to me since I worked as a Starbucks barista for a little more than a year during my seminary days. My supervisors must have known talking to people wasn't my thing, though, because they always put me on the closing shift. Talking to people is my kryptonite. It weakens me and makes me want to fall down. To top it off the barista spelled my name wrong on the cup. Starbucks is kind of like *Cheers*, except instead of remembering your name they misspell it. Signed, Sammie.

A couple of years ago we were in a hard season of life. Our daughter was born with a rare brain condition called Dandy-Walker Syndrome, we moved to a new city, and my father-in-law was dying of multiple myelomas. To deal with the stress, I ate. A lot. I put on twenty pounds, on top of the other twenty I had put on in the previous five years. I was inching toward breaking my own record set in college. The thing about gaining weight is you hope people don't notice, or if they do that they're too nice or oblivious enough not to say anything.

I've only ever wanted to murder someone twice in my life. The first is the counselor I already mentioned. The second was when an older pastor at a prayer meeting told me with a big smirk on his face that I looked like I had been putting on weight. They prayed. I considered where to hide his body.

This same year a friend finally said something to me about my weight. He told me he had been my friend for a long time but had never seen me exercise self-control. Two things in one phrase that I still struggle with, exercise and self-control. My friend said this while in town for a visit, putting words to what I knew was true. My eating was out of control. I was out of control.

So I decided to do something about it. I started running. Really running. At first one mile, then two miles, then three, then four. I wasn't insane, so I stopped there. I started trying to eat healthier. The salad bar from Whole Foods, which means my kids now have enough in their college savings to be home-colleged. Burrito bowls from Chipotle, which now that I think about it, actually does feel like being naked in that you're always a little disappointed at what you see. Lots of fresh fruit and Greek yogurt for breakfast. No fast food. Or fried food. Eating healthy feels like camping. You don't enjoy it; you endure it. And if you enjoy it, something's wrong with you.

My goal was to lose ten pounds in time for a conference where I would see this same friend again in a little less than two months. And I did it. I felt great. People noticed. I couldn't wait to see that friend who had basically told me I was fat and wait for him to say something, anything, that let me know he noticed how much weight I had lost. I finally did and . . . nothing. Not a word. I was crushed. The words I so desperately wanted, needed, to let me know I was okay never came.

There's a scene in *Rudolph the Red Nosed Reindeer* that makes me cry almost every time I watch it. Before Rudolph has been banished to Misfit Island, along with Hermie and others (I still contend that Hermie would have been the most fun dentist ever, but that's for another time), Rudolph is depressed. He feels anything but okay. Then Clarissa says something that changes everything. She tells Rudolph what all of us long to hear. That he's cute. Rudolph is so overwhelmed with joy by these words that he starts shouting it, "I'm cute! I'm cute! She said I'm cute!" For the first time in his reindeer life, he sees himself through the eyes of someone who doesn't just love and accept him, but who delights in him.

I remember watching the movie with my kids during Christmas a few years ago and being overwhelmed by one thought. A question formed in my mind that felt as if it was straight from the heart of God: "What does God think of you?" The way I often talk to myself, I must think he's pretty disappointed with me. Thankfully the gospel tells me differently. Fat or skinny, I am beautiful to God. My weight cannot change my worth. And as good as it feels when someone tells you you're cute, it pales in comparison to the way God feels about you. Here's how God put it to the prophet Isaiah: "As the bridegroom rejoices over the bride, so shall your God rejoice over you" (Isa. 62:5).

When a groom looks at his bride, he thinks two things: "I can't believe how beautiful she is" and "I can't believe she's mine." His joy is in her. She is not just the apple of his eye but the beat of his heart. And that's exactly how the Bible says God feels about his people, about you. G. K. Chesterton wrote of St. Francis of Assisi that "his religion was not a thing like a theory but a thing like a love-affair."[2] The only way that can possibly happen is to have a God so full of love for his people that every day is like his wedding day.

Most of us, though, don't feel beautiful. My friend tells the story about his daughter who loved to dress up in princess dresses and gowns. One day she got a stomach bug and threw up all over her princess dress. As my friend was giving her a bath, she told him with tears in her eyes, "Daddy, I don't feel like a princess anymore."

She didn't understand that it wasn't the dress that made her a princess. It was the love of her dad. There's no such thing as a bride who isn't beautiful on her wedding day. It's not the dress that makes her beautiful. It's the love of the groom. That's what we spend a lifetime learning to believe as Christians. It's not that our beauty makes God love us. It's his love that makes us beautiful.

This is how we can begin to feel okay about ourselves. Our okay-ness isn't dependent upon our weight. It isn't dependent upon someone telling us that we're skinny or that we look really good. Our okay-ness is dependent upon a God whose love makes people beautiful in ways our culture may not value or recognize, but any person with a heart does and will. The beloved of God have a kind of beauty that will never make the cover of *In Style* magazine but will last well into old age and through to eternity.

I'm performing the wedding of a friend soon, and recently we were talking about the vows. As I've said, I'm a fan of traditional vows, not because I'm stuffy, but because I think Thomas Cranmer, archbishop of Canterbury from 1533 to 1556, who wrote the traditional service, was probably a better writer than a couple who wants to rip a page from their moleskin journal and turn it into their vows. My friend agreed. She likes the traditional vows. She just asked if we could add another line. The line? "For skinnier or for fatter."

When my wife started dating me, I was pushing 230

pounds. She kept dating me when I almost hit 250 and stopped wearing underwear so I didn't have to go up to the next size. When she married me, I had dropped down to almost 170. We had both graduated, and I was in a healthier place. The combination of getting off antidepressants and working forty-plus hours a week in landscaping for several months was what caused me to lose weight. I lost so much weight that when we went to visit her grandmother in Michigan for the first time that same summer, she thought her granddaughter had a new fiancé. She had only seen pictures of me. The fat kind.

Actress and comedian Tina Fey wrote in *Bossypants* what she remembered about being skinny and what she remembered about being fat.[3] If I could make my own list, here are a few things it would include.

What I Mainly Remember About Being Skinny

- Trying on, fitting into, and wearing my wife's jeans to the movies
- People not recognizing me :)
- Realizing I had lost an entire second-grader's amount of weight
- Having to punch a new hole at the beginning of my belt because it was way too loose
- All my pants feeling too big
- Having the suits I impulsively bought during college taken in to the point they couldn't be taken in anymore

What I Remember About Being Fat

- People not recognizing me :(
- Realizing I had gained enough weight to have eaten an entire second-grader
- Eating dinner at IHOP, then picking up Wendy's later for a midnight snack
- Punching a hole at the end of my belt because it was way too tight
- Not wearing underwear so I could fit into my pants
- Growing out a mustache and being told I looked like a young Dom DeLuise
- Seeing a picture of myself and ruining a perfectly good day
- Growing a beard not because I love beards but because my face felt fat and naked
- All my pants feeling too tight
- Wishing I had not had those suits taken in

One of the reasons I knew I wanted to marry my wife was that she had seen me at my worst and didn't go anywhere. She knew me at my fattest. She married me at my skinniest. She's seen several versions of both again and again during our eleven years of marriage. There's something beautiful to me about this, something that tells me not that my weight isn't important, but that I'm more than my weight. Her love for me isn't dependent on my appearance, or weighing a certain weight. Her love for me lets me know I'm okay.

But it's just a small picture, a faint smell, a short clip

of the kind of love God has for me. A love that tells me I'm okay, not because I'm okay, but because his love makes me okay. A love that makes me feel more than cute, beautiful even, not because I am, but because in his eyes I am. And a love that is making me more beautiful in a way that will last long after all the magazines have turned to dust.

A year or so ago I decided that I needed a new scale to track my progress as I tried to lose weight. I researched on Amazon and bought one that looked solid and was accurate. It was one of those digital scales made almost entirely of glass. Day after day for weeks and months, I weighed myself. In the morning. At night. After eating a late-night number six combo from Wendy's. I weighed myself constantly. Sometimes I would step off the scale with a smile. Most times I would step off the scale with a scowl, whispering choice words to myself.

A few months ago my wife accidentally dropped the scale on our bathroom floor, and it shattered into a million pieces. I took a picture and put it on Instagram with the caption, "The only thing that would make this better is if it read 'too much shame.'" It wasn't my best work.

Somewhere along the way I got the idea that my worth is directly tied to my weight. More and more I'm getting the idea that my worth can never be measured by a scale. The reality is if I could fit the weight of my worth to God onto a scale, it would smash the scale into a thousand pieces. No scale in the world is fit to handle the weight of our worth as those made in the image of God, precious in his sight.

Your true weight is the weight of your worth to God. It's far too heavy to fit on the scale of your gym. No matter how skinny you get, or how much weight you pack on, the weight of your worth stays the same: infinite.

Chapter Ten

TWEETING OURSELVES TO DEATH

9:52 a.m., Wednesday, December 3, at Drip Coffee

THE ROOM I'M WRITING IN DOUBLES AS A RECORD shop. It's making me want to stop writing and just listen to music. David played music for Saul to calm him down when he had his fits. I could use a David right now. I'm scared about the book. If I hate myself after pretty much every sermon I preach, how in the world am I going to feel about a book? I can take a sermon down from a podcast or, better yet, not put it up in the first place. I can't take books down from a shelf in Barnes & Noble. Has an author ever been arrested for shoplifting his own books from a bookstore so he could burn them? Let me know if you've heard about that happening. Asking for a friend.

One of my friends loves to say that every person you meet is like a book: each has a spine and a story. If that's true then 2013 would make for a page-turner of a chapter in my life, especially the months of April and May. Not everyone can say that the lead-voice actor of Pixar's *Ratatouille* called you a "piece of . . ." (something that typically gets flushed down a toilet). But I can. And I hope with all my heart that makes it into my eulogy.

I joined Twitter in March 2009 (in my head I sound just like Morgan Freeman right now). My first two tweets ever were as follows: "Heading to [some friends' house] for our Bible study cookout . . . hope the potato salad turns out alright. Good times hopefully to be had by all . . ." followed up by "Had a great time at the cookout. Thankful for friends. good times had . . ." Slow down, Hemingway. The Pulitzer committee isn't ready for your envelope-pushing descriptions of potato salad at a cookout.

I quickly moved from looking to tweet the mundane parts of life in painfully boring ways to becoming the next big "gospel tweeter." If you don't know what that is, then you are a normal human being. Don't get me wrong, I still love and follow a lot of guys who mainly use Twitter to share quotes and articles about grace. I love grace. I just sucked at tweeting about it, mainly because I was doing it for all the wrong reasons. Nothing betrays a genuine resting in grace like a desire to be widely known and heavily retweeted. I'm glad Google hasn't debuted a Hidden Motives Translator yet, because all those early tweets would simply read, "Listen, Jesus is great, but I really need this, guys."

Then something strange happened. Two things really. The first was a good friend straight up told me one day,

"You should stop being so serious on Twitter and just try to be funny." By this point I had found @JonAcuff (I think he was still going by @prodigaljohn at the time, the inspiration behind my Twitter handle @prodigalsam). He was the first Christian I ever encountered on Twitter who was really funny; not church-youth-group funny, but could-write-jokes-for-SNL funny. So I listened to my friend and started trying to write funny tweets.

I still remember my first attempt at a joke: "I'd trust a drunken Gary Busey before trusting someone who buys cheap toilet paper." I probably should have just called it quits there, but I kept going. Sort of like that scene in *Forrest Gump* where Forrest starts jogging across the country and people start following him, even though he has no idea where he is going or what he is doing. That's probably the best way to describe how Twitter went for me.

The second thing that happened, and easily the most embarrassing, is I paid money to join this website called *Favstar.fm*. They should change the name to *Internetcrack.fm*, because I was irrepressibly and obsessively hooked. The short version is you pay thirty dollars for a six-month membership so you can give people a virtual trophy for the "Tweet of the Day." It's not as sad as it sounds; it's way sadder. But it was a great way to meet other funny people on Twitter, and I eventually ended up making it to the "Most Popular of Favstar" page, which, in the words of another funny person on Twitter, is "like being a best-selling author in Narnia."[1]

The great thing about Twitter is that it's a safe place to say those things you often think but rarely feel comfortable saying out loud. This is also the terrible thing about Twitter. When the comedian Louis C. K. made a late-night appearance on *Conan*, he elaborated on the difference between calling someone fat to their face versus doing so online. When it's face-to-face, Louis noted, you're forced to watch what it does to the other person. But online, you're solely concerned about what it does to you. And it feels so, so good. It's porn but with words.

Part of his broader point is that the danger of being constantly connected is losing our ability to connect. This was the dark side of Twitter for me, being so connected that I gradually stopped connecting with the most important people in my life. Or as Justin Timberlake, playing Sean Parker, says in the movie *The Social Network*, "We lived on farms, then we lived in cities, and now we're going to live on the Internet." The problem with living on the Internet is that it's not where your family or most of your friends live. They're at home, waiting for you to sit down, look them in the eyes, and connect with them.

I didn't see that because I was so connected that I was losing my ability to connect. My wife did though. We actually got into some pretty big fights about it. My favorites include two separate incidents while we were on vacation. She likes to talk about the first one the most. We were eating at a seafood restaurant at the beach, the kind that spreads out brown paper on the table to soak up the splashing juices. They're great for kids, too, because they give you crayons so you can draw all over the table. I was using those same crayons to scribble down potential tweets on the table that I could use later. Nothing says, "I'm present with you in the moment," like ignoring your family so you can plot out your next tweet to share with complete strangers on the Internet.

I prefer the second incident. We were settling into a beach condo for the week, and we had just put the kids to bed and were headed to the porch to relax when something horrible happened. My wife confessed she hadn't read my blog posts for the last month. I don't remember much after that, except that at some point I screamed, "You don't care about me. You haven't even read my blog posts."

As soon as it came out of my mouth, I knew it sounded ridiculous. But I meant it. And we got into a real fight about it. Not a passive-aggressive I'm-going-to-watch-an-episode-of-our-favorite-show-without-you kind of fight, but a screaming-things-we-had-been-holding-on-to-for-years kind of fight. I was basically looking at the woman who had been my best friend for thirteen years and had loved me through all my different phases (including one where I popped the collar of my pastel polos) and saying she didn't really know me because she hadn't read a couple of things I wrote on the Internet. I was living more online than in reality. In the meantime my family and friends were waiting for me to come back to reality.

One of the dangers of living more online than you do in reality is that you take the people who love you the most for granted, while you pursue the love of people who don't know you, much less love you, at least not the real you. They might love the Twitter you, or the Instagram you, or the Tumblr you; but they don't know the eats-Chick-fil-A-alone-in-your-car you, or the tweeting-before-you-return-their-text you. Your wife does though. Your friends too.

The novelist Jonathan Franzen put this well:

> The simple fact of the matter is that trying to be perfectly likable is incompatible with loving relationships. Sooner or later . . . you're going to find yourself in a hideous, screaming fight, and you'll hear coming out of your mouth things . . . that shatter your self-image as a fair, kind, cool, attractive, in-control, funny, likable person. . . . Suddenly there's a real choice to be made. . . . Do I love this person? And, for the other person, does this person love me?[2]

Franzen's observation reminds me of what one of my best friends told me. We were talking about my newly found Twitter fame, and I was telling him how excited I was one of my Twitter heroes had started following me. (Twitter makes us all sound like cult leaders.) He got serious for a second, a look of concern came over his face, and he said, "You know if you broke your leg, [insert famous Twitter person] wouldn't bring you flowers in the hospital, right?" It felt like your new husband was pouring cold champagne on you on your honeymoon. He was right. I was seeking the approval of complete strangers at the expense of loving the people right in front of me. It didn't stop me though. I kept going.

This is the part of the story that could come across a little arrogant. So to keep it in perspective, think of it as that party on the *Titanic* before they all die. They're dancing and drinking, doing whatever the 1912 version of grinding was, and they have no idea what's about to happen. That was me, minus the making out with Kate Winslet part.

In my wildest dreams I never thought I'd have as many followers on Twitter as I did—130,427 to be exact. But who's counting? I was. It was my self-worth stock market, and I followed it hard. Counting your followers on Twitter is like counting your money in Monopoly: you know it's not ultimately worth anything, yet in that moment it feels like everything. Your credit card may have just been declined at Chipotle, but guess who owns Boardwalk and runs that town like Beyoncé and Jay Z?

Becoming Internet famous did buy some cool things, moments I will work into as many conversations as possible for years to come. ("This rain is really coming down. Speaking of rain, did I ever tell you about that time Rainn Wilson defended me on Twitter?")

But it cost me some things too, namely, my integrity and identity. Sometimes people ask, "How did you do it?" and I typically shrug my shoulders, give some important tipping points and say, "I honestly don't know. It just sort of happened." What I should say is that all you have to do to get a lot of followers on Twitter is figure out who's cool and desperately align yourself with them. Because it's about perception, not reality. It's the "he's with us" of the Internet.

Again, Jonathan Franzen warned about this danger: "One of the worst things about the internet is that it tempts everyone to be a sophisticate—to take positions on what is hip and to consider, under pain of being considered unhip, the positions that everyone else is taking."[3] Integrity is about being the same person, with the same convictions, in any and every situation, with any and every crowd. But it's hard to have convictions when you're constantly wondering if they're cool.

The other danger is looking to the Internet for your identity, instead of the other way around. Internet visionary Jaron Lanier said, "You have to be somebody before you can share yourself."[4] The Internet cannot hold the weight of your identity; only reality can. Twitter became a place for me to be someone else, someone I wanted to be in real life. It's what I call pulling a sad Batman. You change into your alter ego at night, but instead of fighting crime, you're fighting for retweets. Also you don't wake up in a mansion with an amazing car and a butler.

Jon Acuff said, "Fame is a great consequence but a terrible goal."[5] The problem of fame, even the Internet kind, is that you sacrifice knowing yourself for being known. In turn you sacrifice friends for fans. And the reality is all the love in the world means almost nothing when it comes from people who know who you are but don't really know you.

I learned this the hard way. This is where the story gets dark. On the same day an article chronicling my "success" on Twitter broke on *Christianity Today*'s website, another story broke: I was accused of plagiarism. It's a long story, but I was devastated. Comics and writers I love, some of them with millions of followers, made the accusations. A website went up on Tumblr chronicling my theft. Multiple famous comics spread the news. Open letters were written. *Salon* even picked up the story. I was utterly humiliated.

There are so many things I wish I would have done differently. I wish I had owned my faults instead of defending myself. I wish I had apologized for things I did wrong instead of responding out of my hurt. I wish I had not played the victim. I later apologized to specific writers and comics whose permission I felt I should've asked before ever doing tweets similar to theirs. I wish I had done that from the start. Sometimes life is like Hebrew: it's best understood backward.

The end result was that my supervisors asked me to step away from Twitter for six months. I did, and it was the best and hardest six months in a long time. I began writing (more than 140 characters at a time) and started a blog like it was 1999. It was therapeutic, a glimpse of what it could look like to be on the Internet not as a caricature but as myself. I had used humor to serve myself and build a following. I was a pastor trying to become a comedian. What could it look like to be a pastor who uses humor in a way that is honest and life-giving to others? I knew it would mean that I would no longer be afraid to be myself, a husband, father, pastor, believer, and very amateur humorist, instead of hiding behind the image of @prodigalsam, a character with grandiose (selfish) dreams of leaving the ministry for Hollywood.

During the six-month break, a Facebook friend (the irony isn't lost on me) reached out to say he was sorry for what I was going through, and that he'd gone through something similar. During that season he had read a book that had helped him tremendously. He asked if he could send it to me. He did. That book was Walter Brueggemann's *Spirituality of the Psalms,*[6] and I couldn't put it down.

In his book, Brueggemann says that the psalms basically take three different shapes. There are psalms of orientation, where we are praising God for how good life is. Then there are psalms of disorientation, where we are asking God how he could bring something so painful into our lives. Out of those psalms grow what he calls psalms of reorientation, where God is putting a new song on our lips and changing us from the inside out. This is the same pattern found in Jesus' life: life, death, and resurrection. Jesus said that would be the pattern of all his followers.

The season I was in was one of complete disorientation. How could God allow me to be so completely and publicly humiliated? What possible good could come from any of this? The answer, of course, wasn't found in what God was doing (or would do) for me. It was found in what God was doing in me. Changing me from someone who was wrecking his life for the approval of strangers, turning me into someone who was content with who I am: loved by God, family, children, friends, and fellow travelers. I am somebody. Sometimes I forget this. I'm at my best when I remember.

Margaret Atwood wrote, "When you are in the middle of a story it isn't a story at all, but only a confusion; a dark roaring, a blindness, a wreckage of shattered glass and splintered wood. . . . It's only afterwards that it becomes anything like a story at all. When you are telling it, to yourself or to someone else."[7]

My hope for this dark roaring part of my life is that it could become a story worth telling. In some ways it's a story of warning; how not to do the Internet. In other ways, at least for me, it's also a story of redemption. Those are the stories it seems God loves to tell. The ones that have messy middles but beautiful endings. The ones that bear the marks of grace, which always surprises, interrupts, and subverts our agendas.

3:27 p.m., Thursday, December 4, at
home, with a cold cup of coffee

TRYING TO WRITE WITH KIDS AROUND IS ONE FUN WAY of never wanting to write again ever. Can't they see Dad is busy with something far more important than closing the laptop and spending time with them? He's writing the thing that's going to keep us from ending up sharing beds with grandparents like Charlie and his family in *Willie Wonka and the Chocolate Factory*. I show my kids that scene every morning to keep us all motivated. Just kidding. I show them *The Shining* instead so they'll know what will happen if they keep bothering Daddy. Honestly I'm afraid what writing a book could do to me as a dad. I don't want to be the dad who cares more about being something or someone than about being a dad. I don't want to put my kids on the back burner while I give all my attention to this thing I think will satisfy me. Hold that thought. The kids are fighting, and I need to go yell, "Guys. *Guys.* Guys. *Guys.* You guys. Guys," over and over at my kids. It's my only parenting move. Unless you count Netflix.

After the six-month break I debated on whether I should come back to Twitter. I got all kinds of advice, mostly along the lines of don't come back, come back and don't change, and come back and change. I chose door number three, having no idea what would happen once I opened it. There was an initial wave of both excitement and disgust. My third tattoo idea is to have Jesus' words about approval tattooed on my knuckles so I have to see them every time I'm about to send a tweet: "Woe to you, when all people speak well of you" (Luke 6:26).

Things are a little different now. I'm a little more myself, I hope. I'm a little less caught in the cycle of desperately trying to be funny so that I can feel a wave of approval wash over me. That's the biggest lesson I learned. Approval is a lover who will always break your heart. And in terms of approval, the Internet is a seductive place.

Part of this is because the Internet makes approval feel more tangible. No one in real life can like or star or retweet something you say. The best they can do is laugh a little harder, smile a little bigger. Not so with the Internet. The approval you feel is instantly measured by how much a post is shared, liked, "favorited," or reposted. The danger of posting something online for me lies in the way I track its reception like a new iPhone about to be delivered to my doorstep: obsessively and compulsively. I want to feel the rush of approval.

In the movie *Birdman*, Michael Keaton is a former blockbuster action-movie hero turned struggling actor in his late career. He thinks if he can just pull off a successful run on Broadway, his career will be redeemed. At one point Amy Ryan, his ex-wife, looks at him backstage after one of the shows and says something that cut straight to my heart: "That's what you always do. You confuse love for admiration."

The seductive lie of approval is that if enough people like you, you will feel loved and accepted, made whole. The problem is that you can never really know if someone really likes you (you're not omniscient), and even if they do, you can never guarantee they will keep doing so (you're not omnipotent either). To paraphrase something I read by Shauna Niequist, the Internet makes you feel liked by people who can't love you because they don't really know you, have never really met you. The Internet is a great place to buy vintage T-shirts, but it is a terrible place to look for love.

My dad is fond of saying, "What you think of me is none of my business." I used to hate it when he said this. Now I realize he's right. What you think of me is none of my business. And if we're being honest, you probably don't think of me very much at all. David Foster Wallace noted this directly in *Infinite Jest*: "You will become way less concerned with what other people think of you when you realize how seldom they do."[8]

The only one whose thoughts about me I can really know is God. "Jesus loves me this I know, for the Bible tells me so" remains one of the most profound truths ever penned. The apostle Paul, when reflecting on his lack of concern of what others thought of him, rooted it in his knowledge that Jesus "loved me and gave himself for me" (Gal. 2:20). How do I know that he loves me? Because he gave himself for me. The cross is tangible proof that God literally loves you to death. One look at the cross, and you can know exactly what God thinks about you.

None of this keeps me from struggling with approval. Just the other day I wrote and then deleted three tweets because they got the Internet version of "crickets." I knew as I posted them that I was more doing it mostly because I was feeling a little down and hoped a little fix of Internet approval would help. It didn't. It never does. One of the ways I know I shouldn't be online is when I'm looking to get something that I already have in abundance as a child of God. It's on days like that when I have to remind myself that even if my post gets zero likes, I am still 100 percent loved. All the approval I ever need is sitting at the right hand of God.

Chapter Eleven

SIDE-HUGGING JESUS

8:47 a.m., Monday, December 15, at Starbucks

CONFESSION: I'VE HAD MY HEADPHONES ON FOR A solid couple of hours without any music playing. Apparently I'm not above pretending to sip from an empty cup of coffee just to prove I'm worthy of keeping this table. My ability to simultaneously be afraid of people while deeply trying to please them is my superpower. Getting close to finishing the book, and it feels surreal. The main thought I can't shake is what are my friends and my family going to think. Any time they ask me what the book is about, imagine a dog being shocked by an electric collar because that's exactly what I look like. Have I shared too much? Will it come across as narcissistic? Can everyone just skip the chapter on lust? As much as I say vulnerability is where we meet God and one another, honestly I'd rather we just meet at Starbucks and pretend to connect about shows we're currently watching on Netflix. I hope Jesus is ready to talk about *Friday Night Lights* when I meet him.

It's no coincidence that around the time I got obsessed with Twitter, my wife and I had just learned that our little girl who was about to be born had a rare condition called Dandy-Walker Syndrome, a congenital brain malformation involving the cerebellum. Fluid buildup was putting pressure on her little brain, and the doctors couldn't tell us what it all meant, except that she would either be okay or very sick. The not knowing was the hardest part.

Sadie was born and, to our inexplicable joy, seemed to be okay. Her condition, however, meant that we were regulars at the hospital for a while. Just a few months after Sadie was born, we were back at the hospital delivering her to surgery while we anxiously waited. Our pediatric neurosurgeon told us that she needed a shunt to help drain the excess fluid from her brain, a tube that would run from the front of her brain, behind her ear, beside her chest, to where it emptied out into her stomach, like a river winding its way through her little body, making her life possible.

I remember doing two things on Twitter that day. The first was to ask for prayer. We were nervous and had no idea what to expect. Also we had to eat hospital food, which actually tastes like food that's sick. The second was to tell some really lame jokes in an attempt, I think, to make myself laugh in the face of a painful situation. Laughter reminds us we're not alone, that sad things don't ultimately have the final say.

I tweeted things like, "It's really fun to make eye contact with one of the doctors, wink, and then mouth 'You're my McDreamy,'" which really isn't funny, but I remember the chair I was sitting in as I wrote it, and how thinking of jokes took my mind off of the scalpels that at the moment were bearing down on my daughter's doll-sized body to place a tube in her that will be there as long as she lives.

The shunt saved her life. Literally. It helps her function like a totally normal, healthy, happy little girl. All we have to do is make sure the shunt is draining like it should. Not too much. Not too little. Modern medicine is a beautiful thing for which we are thankful.

Her shunt is also a reminder that there is one thing you can never protect your kids from: suffering. They are born into this world, and you hope so many things for them. Deep friendships, happy marriages, satisfying careers, love for Jesus and his people. And you work your hardest to give them the good and protect them from the bad. They are yours, your friends, your prisoners,[1] for a short season before you send them wide-eyed into this world.

But as hard as you try, you can't protect them from the suffering they will inevitably experience by virtue of being broken people in a broken world. All you can do is teach them how to suffer well, to suffer knowing that somehow God knows best, does good, works good, is good, both in and through the suffering. And in those moments when you cannot trace his hand, you can still trust his heart.[2]

If you went back to Facebook around the time we found out the hard news about our little girl, you would find the following quote from novelist and essayist Marilynne Robinson on my wall: "That is how life goes—we send our children into the wilderness. Some of them on the day they are born, it seems, for all the help we can give them. Some of them seem to be a kind of wilderness unto themselves. But there must be angels there, too, and springs of water. Even that wilderness, the very habitation of jackals, is the Lord's."[3]

The Lord doesn't promise to never take us into the wilderness. This is the bad news. The good news is that even the wilderness is his, and he is there.

This is what makes life such a scary place to live though. It's the place where we get hurt. It's the place where we are abandoned and feel betrayed. It's the place where, as hard as we might try, we can never be safe and in control. Things happen, some good, some bad, all just beyond our ability to control them. This is what I think the fortune-teller in the movie *Before Sunrise* meant when she told the happy couple to resign themselves to the awkwardness of life. Life's awkwardness lies in the fact that we can never quite mold it to our own safe purposes. No matter how much we try to keep things in order, life seems determined to scatter Legos under our bare feet.

My counselor once guided me through an exercise in which I mapped out all the places in my life where I had been traumatically hurt or disappointed. He called it my "trauma egg" because it detailed the places where my fears and insecurities hatched. Now that I think about it, it sounds like the worst Easter egg hunt of all time. Unless the Easter eggs are filled with Whoppers, then I think I'd actually rather take the trauma egg because Whoppers taste like you're eating a really old person covered in chocolate.

In that session my counselor said something that will always stick with me. He told me that even though I was a pastor who talked with people all the time about trusting God, I was afraid to trust him myself. He was right. I can give you all the reasons you should trust God; about how he is sovereign over every molecule, counts the number of hairs on your head, knows when even a sparrow falls to the ground, and is working everything, good and bad, for your good and his glory. But if I'm being honest, I still would rather be in control because at least then I would know how and when I might get hurt. Trusting God might be simple, but it's far from easy.

It makes me think of the scene in the movie *Two Towers* when Smeagol enters the Forbidden Pool at Gondor to catch a few fish to eat. Frodo goes to fetch him from the pool before Faramir's men pierce him with arrows. He reaches out his hand, saying, "Smeagol. Master is here. Come, Smeagol. Trust master. Come." Smeagol senses something is wrong, but reluctantly listens to Frodo and follows him. The moment he does, the men of Gondor rush in and bind him with chains. The look on Smeagol's face is one of absolute heartbreak. How could master do this to us?

I know the look on Smeagol's face, the one that screams, "If you love me, how could you do this to me?" You do too. It's the one that comes when God doesn't answer our prayers the way we want, doesn't seem to even hear them.

It's the one that comes when well-meaning people tell us it will work out and it doesn't. Not even close. It's the one that comes when well-meaning people are trite about our suffering, pretending they understand it, quoting Romans 8:28 ("And we know that for those who love God all things work together for good, for those who are called according to his purpose") in a way that makes you want to punch them in the throat.

Flannery O'Connor wrote, "A God you understood would be less than yourself."[4] This is precisely what Job found out when he finally got his meeting with God. He didn't get answers for his suffering. Instead he got a bigger view of God, which itself is a kind of answer. Our comfort in suffering isn't in understanding it, but in believing there's a God far bigger than ourselves who does. He asks us to trust him. He knows it's hard.

My mom had a charcoal drawing of Jesus holding a lamb in his arms. Jesus is laying his head on the lamb's as it peacefully rests on his shoulder. It's a beautiful picture, but I have an idea for one that might more realistically capture my relationship with Jesus. It's a charcoal drawing of a lamb side-hugging Jesus, as if to say, "I love you, but keep your distance. I've heard about what happens to lambs." Maybe this explains why Christians are so good at side hugs. We're pros when it comes to loving Jesus but asking him to keep his distance.

The good news is that Jesus didn't keep his distance, and he still doesn't. He drew near to us by becoming human and suffering for us in order that he might suffer with us. Because he did, our suffering isn't without meaning, even if its only meaning is to somehow make us more like him. This is better news than what's found in the poem "Footprints in the Sand," because it means he's doing something loving and good even in those places where it seems he's not so much carrying us but dragging us through sand.

Martin Luther used to talk about the difference between what he called a "theology of glory" and a "theology of the cross." When we first become a Christian, we have this idea that from here on out, life is supposed to become a little better, a little easier. It's the scene in the movie after the character has had an epiphany, or a wonderful experience, and he's walking through a crowd of people, and they start singing, and the animals start singing too. That's our vision of what life should be like after we become a Christian. This, Luther said, is a theology of glory. The problem is that there is no glory without the cross.

A theology of the cross is different. Bad things happen to good people. Good things happen to bad people. Jesus was crucified while Pilate enjoyed Roman luxury at its finest. Pastor Matt Chandler says that following God can end badly. The cross, far from being some charm that makes everything suddenly sweet, is a symbol of the death that God brings into the lives of his beloved. This means the way to glory is through the path of suffering. It's in the seasons of suffering that our hearts are most revealed to us.

If we operate out of a theology of glory, it means we will be confused when suffering and sadness come our way. We will think God must not love us or he wouldn't do such things, bring such things into our lives. We miss the part in Romans

8 that says the glorious things God is doing are now and not yet. He does glorious things. Yet we groan for him to do yet more as we wait for the day when he finally and eternally will.

If we operate out of a theology of the cross, we know that part of God's love is to make us like Jesus in the sufferings of his life and death. He's taking the rough block of wood that is ourselves, and he's carving away everything that isn't Jesus. His sharpest tools are the ones that strip away the idols we cling to with clenched fists.

It's easy to want to give yourself to a God of glory, because he's less a God and more like the pillow I lay my head on every night. I love my pillow. It exists to provide me comfort. It has no other purpose. Except maybe when it's fluffed and placed perfectly on our bed to make it look ready for a *Southern Living* photo shoot. That's how some of us think about Jesus. Jesus exists to comfort me and to make my life look better.

It's a lot harder to want to give yourself to a God of the cross, because you know his will for you might not be your will for you. Worse yet, you know his will for you involves suffering and heartbreak. He never promises us a life free of suffering. He does promise us something better. He will be with us. The problem is we don't really want God. We want a pillow. We want something to make us feel better, not tell us what to do while messing up our lives.

2:32 p.m., Friday, December 19, at Drip Coffee

I'M SO READY TO FINISH THIS BOOK. AND YET I'M SO not ready to finish this book. I've always been a quitter. Diets.

Exercise plans. JV Football. Jobs. College, almost. I've quit a lot. I'd like to quit writing right now and go smoke, even though I don't really smoke except occasionally with smoker-friends because I want them to like me. Don't most writers smoke? I can see why. It gives you something to do with your hands that makes you feel cool. Because writing doesn't. Writing makes you feel anything but cool because you know people are going to read your words, and quite a few of them are going to put them down because they think you're a bad writer. I can feel myself having a tiny panic attack as I type. Is it too late to stop writing this book? Like Jake Gyllenhaal kinda said in *Brokeback Mountain*, I wish I knew how to quit you, book.

The more I think about my own story, especially my intimacy with Jesus, the more convinced I am that this is what happened. At first it was easy to trust him because he hadn't yet brought anything painful into my life. The irony is that it was something incredibly painful, my parent's divorce, that brought me to him in the first place, that caused me to cry out. But I wanted glory. I wanted my life to be easy, hashtag blessed. And I wanted to be better than everyone else. I would never have said that I thought I was better than everyone else. But I thought it. And my variety of matching WWJD bracelets said it for me.

Instead Jesus brought suffering, in the words of John Newton, to show me "the hidden evils of my heart."[5] The problem is that the more suffering Jesus brings into our lives, the harder it is to trust him. Not because he isn't trustworthy and faithful. But because he can't be trusted to do only the things that we approve of, that we want him to do. We want God to be a "yes" man. A friend who only does what we want and never disagrees with our plans. The problem is if he were that kind of friend, he would cease to be God.

One of the first things that Jesus' best friend John said about him was that he was full of grace and truth. These are the very things that make us afraid of Jesus. We can't handle his truth, and we're afraid of receiving his grace. What are supposed to be comforts to a splintered soul, the very things that can make us whole, in reality, terrify us.

We're afraid of his truth because he knows the truth about us. There's no hiding from him, no covering up our imperfections. He knows us through and through, to the bottom. And he's not afraid to tell us the truth about what we need and what we don't. He isn't too sentimental in his friendship with us to never utter sharp words of rebuke. Neither is he afraid to tell us what to do. There's no one who knows what we need and what we need to do better than Jesus. He is so full of truth he could never lie to us, even in the places we wish he would.

We're afraid of his grace too. It makes us just like everybody else: sinners in need of forgiveness. We don't want to be like everybody else. We want to be special, more put together. Because then we can know we're important. Then we can know we're okay. We also know that if grace is true, it means there isn't a part of our lives that is off limits to him. He is in complete control. We are completely at his mercy. We would rather have God in our debt than be in his. Our self-sufficiency makes grace seem more like a threat than a cure.

The reason we fail to talk about the things we need to talk about most is because those are the very things we don't know how to talk to Jesus about. How do you talk to Jesus about your lust? Your depression? Your parents' divorce? Your loneliness? The hard parts of your marriage? The way you hate yourself?

We're afraid of him telling us the truth, and we're afraid he won't be gracious. The good news is the Lord is not harsh with us. His truth comes dripping in grace. Neither is he gracious without offering us guidance and wisdom. He is true in his words and true in his ways. God loves to speak truth to his children. He loves to be gracious to them as well. If he isn't doing both, then you don't have the real God in your life.

There's a story from priest and author Henri Nouwen's life that I love. He was leading a chapel service and felt compelled by Jesus to turn it into a healing touch service. As the people gathered, settling down into their chairs, he invited them to come forward if they would like to be hugged and to be reminded of the love of God for them. It's no accident that Jesus' ministry was full of healing touch. Nouwen wanted this service to be a glimpse of the healing grace of Jesus' embrace. Every single person seated in the room came forward. Nouwen hugged them and spoke the promises of God's grace over them.

As the last person came forward, Nouwen noticed a janitor in the back of the room. He had been watching the service, probably unsure what to make of it at first. Then as he began to watch, his heart was drawn. And as the last person sat back down, he simply raised his hand and asked, "Me too?" Nouwen invited him forward, embraced him, and spoke the love of Christ over him.

The good news is that Jesus doesn't give side hugs. He always invites me into the fullness of his embrace. He's never unsure of what to do with me. Because he knows me, I don't have to hide. Because he died for me, I don't have to cover. Because he is the Good Shepherd, he knows what to do with lambs. Because he is the Lamb of God, they are always safe in his arms. Because he knew suffering, he knows how to comfort me. Because his suffering had cosmic purpose, he knows what to do with my suffering.

I still struggle to believe this. Trusting God became hard the day my dad left. The way I felt finding out about Sadie's condition was eerily similar to how I felt the day I learned my dad wasn't coming home. If your dad left, who won't leave? No person, no relationship is safe. Where was God when my dad walked away? The questions my twelve-year-old heart was asking, my thirty-year-old heart still couldn't answer. Sadie's complications were just another goodie to stuff in the trauma egg alongside my dad's leaving.

A few years ago I was processing my "dad story" with a friend in Starbucks, and he said something that made me openly sob. You haven't experienced awkwardness until you've openly cried in Starbucks. I know, because, as I shared earlier, I've done it a lot. I'll never forget what he said: "Sammy, if you're ever going to get healthy, adult Sammy is going to have to go back to twelve-year-old Sammy, take his hand, look him in the eye, and tell him, 'Dad's not coming home.'"

My eyes became a sprinkler of tears, so many tears the other customers must have thought I was listening to Bon Iver's cover of Bonnie Raitt's "I Can't Make You Love Me."

The reason I started crying in Starbucks wasn't the sadness of what my friend was saying. What made me cry was a small voice that I could almost hear saying, "Yes. And I want to take you by the hand, and go with you, and weep with you there." Jesus isn't indifferent to our suffering. He wept when his friend Lazarus died, not because he was putting on a good show, or because he was sentimental, or because he couldn't do anything about his death. He wept because he loved his friend and felt the pain of suffering, even a suffering he was about to undo. When the apostle Paul tells us to "weep with those who weep," all he's really telling us to do is be like Jesus (Rom. 12:15).

There's a scene in C. S. Lewis's *The Magician's Nephew* that is my favorite scene in the entire Chronicles of Narnia series. Digory, the young boy in the story, has a mother who is dying. All he wants is for Aslan to make her well. He pleads with Aslan:

> "But please, please—won't you—can't you give me something that will cure Mother?" Up till then he had been looking at the Lion's great feet and the huge claws on them; now, in his despair, he looked up at its face. What he saw surprised him as much as anything in his whole life. For the tawny face was bent down near his own and (wonder of wonders) great shining tears stood in the Lion's eyes. They were such big, bright tears

compared with Digory's own that for a moment he felt as if the Lion must really be sorrier about his Mother than he was himself.[6]

Recently I was putting Sadie to bed, and as we were lying there, waiting for her to fall asleep, I could tell she was thinking about something. So I asked her what she was thinking about. She said, "I have two dads." I braced myself for the next thing out of her mouth to be either super weird, or super devastating about my wife. "You're my dad and God is my dad." Sprinkler tears again shot from my eyes.

One day when she's old enough, I'm going to give her a recording of the first sermon I preached after we learned that she had Dandy-Walker, before we knew what it would look like for her. It was centered on one small verse in one of the smallest books of the Bible about one of the least-known prophets, Nahum: "The LORD is good, a stronghold in the day of trouble; he knows those who take refuge in him" (Nah. 1:7).

Her Father is the only hope for her father. His goodness runs through all that he is and does. He doesn't promise a safe journey. But he does promise to be a mountain of safety when the journey gets rough. Because he knew me before the foundation of the world, even when the foundation of the world seems to shake in confusion, he knows what he is doing with me, in me, through me, and for me, awkwardness and all.

The good news is that the Lord loves awkward people, for there isn't any other kind.

ACKNOWLEDGMENTS

To Wolgemuth & Associates and Nelson Books: thank you for believing in this project, for being so supportive and helpful, and for not making me hate "the man" more.

To Erik Wolgemuth: thank you for guiding me through this entire at times pant-wetting experience.

To Webb Younce: thank you for your kind words, your sense of humor, and your impeccable ability to take a manuscript and make it much, much better.

To my high school English teachers Mrs. Diane McKenzie and Mrs. Sharon Young: I wasn't the best writer or the best student, but your love of books was infectious, and you infected me with the sheer joy of good books, even half-read ones. Thank you.

To my RUF family: thank you for the outpouring of love, grace, wisdom, and support over the last ten years. I showed up as an outsider and you were kind enough to bring me in and help me learn to talk about the parts of life that are hard. This book is the fruit of your kindness and faithfulness to me.

To my students: thank you for being patient with me as I wrote, and for trusting me to hold your stories well. Thank you, too, for not giving up on me even after I repeatedly failed to respond to your texts.

To my friends and family: thank you for being the "V" from Shel Silverstein's poem "Love": constantly showing up in love even when it doesn't suit you. Special thanks to Tim Udouj and Emily Whitley for taking the time to read the rough, rough draft and giving me helpful feedback.

To my sister: thank you for making it fun to be a brother, and for being a voice of encouragement in my life. Also for letting me vent about Mom and Dad on the runs I so look forward to between visits.

To my mom: thank you for being a rock to me, and for loving me with a never-giving-up kind of love. This book would not be possible if it were not for your strength and love. Thank you for teaching me not to give up no matter how tough or long the row.

To my dad: thank you for your honesty, your humor, and your love of writing. Thank you for being an open book, and for being not just my dad, but my friend. Let's keep making up for lost time.

To my Jayne Mac, Asher, Eloise, and Sadie: thank you for letting me be your dad, and for forgiving me when I fall short of being the kind of dad you need. You know the real me and still love me. I love you more than I know how to show or say. I'm working on it.

To my wife, Alyssa: we said "I do" twelve years ago and there have been a lot of "I don't"s between then and now. Thank you for being patient with my crazy, and for loving me in my awkward. All the laughter, the tears, the shouts, and the whispers have been aging our marriage into a wine that tastes ever better as the years go on. You are my best friend and I love you deeply still.

Appendix A

AN INTROVERT'S GUIDE TO SURVIVING A PARTY

Very few things are harder on introverts than parties. Your friend doing that thing where she wraps a criticism in the form of a question. Your other friend doing that thing where he confuses talking football with emotionally connecting. So much small talk, so little access to a doctor friend who recklessly prescribes Xanax. It's all so overwhelming. But take heart, my introverted friend. Here are a few quick tips on surviving that party:

1. *Bathrooms make great panic rooms.*

Your attackers? Upbeat people pummeling you with question after question, story after story. Your refuge? That glorious eight-by-ten-foot space filled with old *Southern Living* magazines, better known as "introvert paradise." So lock the door, and take a seat and a deep breath. Worst-case scenario, your friends think you have a sickness or struggle you haven't told them about. This can actually work in your favor.

2. *Reward yourself for eye contact.*

Any personal trainer will tell you that the key to exercise success is rewarding yourself with food. Okay, that's not true. But food does make for a great eye contact motivator at a party. Here's how it works. Five seconds of eye contact equals another handful of Chex mix. Fifteen seconds of eye contact equals another dessert. Thirty seconds of eye contact equals—slow down, Katie Couric, let's take this one baby-step at a time.

3. *Keep your phone out as much as possible.*

Get some group messages started about that recent friend drama. Or start a debate about education on Facebook with friends who have radically different views. Pin some new workout routines or cake recipes on Pinterest. Snapchat yourself being bored. Anything to distract you from actual human interaction. An introvert's iPhone is like Batman's utility belt. Use it wisely. Use it well.

4. *Bring a pair of oversized headphones.*

Dogs are man's best friend, but not if you're an introvert. Then an embarrassingly big pair of headphones are. How do you let someone know you're not interested in talking to them without saying a word? By bringing, and never, ever taking off, a pair of oversized headphones. Never mind that they make your hair look more matted than the hair of a college freshman who hasn't showered in a few weeks. The lack of social engagement will be more than worth it.

5. *Don't say goodbye. Just ghost.*

That's the exact advice of *Slate* contributor, Seth Stevenson.[1] And it's the best party advice an introvert could ever receive. All those awkward side hugs and halfhearted goodbyes can wait until next year. As actress Jenny Mollen tweeted, "My favorite part of every party is leaving." Amen. So go sink into the front seat of your Jetta or minivan, put on some depressing music, and gently high-five or weep to yourself because you just survived every introvert's worst nightmare: a party.

A SOCIAL MEDIA MANIFESTO

L ook up the definition of *manifesto* online, and you'll find something along the lines of the following: "a written statement that describes the policies, goals, and opinions of a person or group." This is an attempt at a personal (short) manifesto about how to live our lives online.

1. *Don't share more online than you share in your real life.*

We all know someone who's a chronic over-sharer online. Many of us have been that person. Why? In *Daring Greatly*, Brené Brown gives us a warning about real vs. false vulnerability. She says, "Boundaryless disclosure is one way we protect ourselves from real vulnerability. . . . [V]ulnerability is bankrupt on its own terms when people move from *being* vulnerable to *using* vulnerability to deal with unmet needs, get attention, or engage in the shock-and-awe behaviors that are so commonplace in today's culture."[1] Don't be more vulnerable online than you are in real life with real friends.

2. *Real-life friends always have priority over online friends.*

Not every conversation needs to be mined for tweetable nuggets. Not every party needs to be Instagrammed. Not every facial expression needs to be Snapchatted. Most of the time we need to simply put away our phones and be with our friends. If our online habits are a distraction or a destruction to real-life friendships, we need to rethink them.

3. *Practice empathy in all your online interactions.*

This is what Louis C. K. was getting out during his appearance on *Conan.* Insulting online lets you get all the good parts of how it made you feel without the hard parts of how it made the other person feel. If "the words of a whisperer are like delicious morsels" (Prov. 18:8), then online comments are like an all-you-can-eat buffet. Never say anything online you don't first imagine yourself saying to someone's face.

4. *Work hard at using social media to enhance your real life, not escape it.*

Author and speaker Seth Godin said, "Instead of wondering when your next vacation is, maybe you should set up a life you don't need to escape from."[2] The same applies for the way we do life online. How can we use Facebook, Twitter, and Instagram to connect instead of becoming increasingly disconnected?

5. *Carefully watch your "people I wish I knew" to "people I already know" interaction ratio.*

This one especially applies to Twitter when your favorite famous person is just an @ away. The danger here is beginning to lose yourself in an attempt to be-"friend" a person (or group of people) you don't really know. The more disconnected your life online becomes from your real life, the more disconnected you will be from the real people in your life. The Internet is like Waffle House: it makes everyone, celebrities included, seem approachable (also it makes you feel dirty). The danger of this is you can use the Internet as a way to stop connecting with the people who know and love you already.

6. *Talk about your online life with real-life friends.*

Only your real friends can help you from pulling a Sad Batman. You need real friends who can lovingly rebuke and speak into your online presence. You need to have a couple of friends you're regularly talking to about the temptations and interactions happening in your online life. This seems like a weird thing to say, I know. But we need friends who say things to us like this: I really enjoyed that blog post, but your goal for today is not to check it every five minutes to see how many likes it got. One of my best friends did this for me recently and I loved him so much for it.

7. *You're worth far more than your follower count.*

All the love in the world means almost nothing when it comes from people who know who you are but don't actually know you. Trust me. If you measure your worth in retweets and likes, favorites and followers, you will never measure up, because you're only as good as your last post. You'll never be enough. But if you measure your worth by your preciousness to God and a growing nearness to the people who love you, you can rest easy in the knowledge that you are enough for them. They love you for who you are, not for who you're trying to be. I've always loved the way C. S. Lewis said it in *Prince Caspian*: "You come from the Lord Adam and the Lady Eve," said Aslan. "And that is both honour enough to erect the head of the poorest beggar, and shame enough to bow the shoulders of the greatest emperor on earth. Be content."[3]

NOTES

INTRODUCTION

1. John Updike, *Self-Consciousness: Memoirs* (New York: Random House, 2012), 250.
2. Anne Lamott (@annelamott) on Twitter, 8:16 p.m., April 23, 2012, https://twitter.com/annelamott/status/194580559962439681.

CHAPTER 1: DON'T WASTE YOUR AWKWARDNESS

1. Anne Lamott on Twitter, 1:51 a.m., July 26, 2012, https://twitter.com/annelamott/status/228366902668439552.
2. Adam Kotsko, *Awkwardness: An Essay* (Ropley, Hants, U.K: John Hunt Publishing, 2010). I first read about this idea, and parts of this list, in Kotsko's super helpful book.
3. Brené Brown, "Listening to Shame," TED, March 2012, http://www.ted.com/talks/brene_brown_listening_to_shame/transcript?language=en.
4. C. John Miller, *Repentance: A Daring Call to Real Surrender* (Fort Washington, PA: CLC Publications, 1975, 1980, 2009), 85.

5. This idea comes from Timothy Keller, "The Gospel and Your Self," preached at Redeemer Presbyterian Church, Manhattan, NY, November 13, 2005.
6. John Calvin, *The Institutes of the Christian Religion*, trans. Henry Beveridge (Peabody, MA: Hendrickson Publishers, 2008), 5.
7. Kotsko, *Awkwardness: An Essay*, n.p.

CHAPTER 2: PARENTS ARE A GIFT

1. Or, as Ben Stiller says it in the movie *Greenberg*, "Hurt people hurt people."
2. Dan Allender, *How Children Raise Parents: The Art of Listening to Your Family* (Colorado Springs: Waterbrook Press, 2003), 21.
3. The result on the viewer is equally devastating because it's almost impossible to bear seeing Coach Taylor (Kyle Taylor's most loved role) from *Friday Night Lights* in this way.
4. Michael Chabon, *Manhood for Amateurs: The Pleasures and Regrets of a Husband, Father, and Son* (New York: HarperCollins, 2010), 7.
5. John Newton and Richard Cecil, *The Select Works of The Rev. John Newton* (Edinburgh: Peter Brown and Thomas Nelson, 1831), 288.
6. William M. Struthers, *Wired for Intimacy: How Pornography Hijacks the Male Brain* (Downers Grove, IL: InterVarsity Press, 2009), 150.
7. Michael Chabon, *Telegraph Avenue: A Novel* (New York: HarperCollins, 2012), 10.
8. James K. A. Smith, "Letter to a Young Parent," http://www .cardus.ca/comment/article/2804/letter-to-a-young-parent/.
9. Anne Lamott, *Bird by Bird: Some Instructions on Writing and Life* (New York: Anchor Books, 1995), 28.

CHAPTER 3: *D* IS FOR DIVORCE

1. Sarah Seltzer, "Five Flannery O'Connor Quotes to Live By," Flavorwire, http://flavorwire.com/511277/5-flannery-oconnor -quotes-to-live-by.
2. Judith S. Wallerstein, Julia M. Lewis, and Sandra Blakeslee, *The Unexpected Legacy of Divorce: A 25 Year Landmark Study* (New York: Hyperion, 2000), 316.
3. Melvin Maddocks, "Books: Out of the Woods," *Time Magazine*, March 19, 1973, xx, http://content.time.com/time /magazine/article/0,9171,906966,00.html.
4. Teddy Roosevelt, "Citizenship in a Republic," Paris, France, April 23, 1910, http://design.caltech.edu/erik/Misc/Citizenship _in_a_Republic.pdf.
5. Eric Metaxas, *Bonhoeffer: Pastor, Martyr, Prophet, Spy* (Nashville: Thomas Nelson, 2010), 458.

CHAPTER 4: THE PORN IN MY SIDE

1. C. S. Lewis, *Mere Christianity* (New York: HarperCollins, 1952), 143.
2. Dan Allender, *The Wounded Heart: Hope for Adult Victims of Childhood Sexual Abuse* (Colorado Springs: NavPress, 2008), 140.
3. C. S. Lewis, *The Four Loves* (New York: Harcourt Brace, 1960), 56.
4. Russell Brand, "My Life without Drugs," *The Guardian*, March 19, 2013, http://www.theguardian.com/culture/2013 /mar/09/russell-brand-life-without-drugs.
5. Dallas Willard, *Renovation of the Heart: Putting on the Character of Christ* (Colorado Springs: NavPress, 2002), 240.
6. David Foster Wallace, *Infinite Jest* (New York: Back Bay Books, 1996), 235.
7. Brené Brown, "Listening to Shame," TED, March 2012, http:// www.ted.com/talks/brene_brown_listening_to_shame.

8. G. K. Chesterton, *Orthodoxy* (New York and London: John Lane Co., 1909), 223.
9. C. S. Lewis, *The Problem of Pain* (New York: HarperCollins, 1940, 1996), 95–96.

CHAPTER 5: *D* IS ALSO FOR DEPRESSION

1. Martin Luther, *The Table Talk of Martin Luther*, ed. William Hazlitt (London: Bell & Daldy, 1872), 317.
2. D. Martyn Lloyd-Jones, The Christian Warfare (Grand Rapids: Baker Books, 1976), 206–208.
3. Jeffrey Eugenides, *The Marriage Plot* (New York: Macmillan, 2011), 259–60.
4. David Foster Wallace, "The Planet Trillaphon As It Stands in Relation to the Bad Thing," *The Amherst Review* 12 (1984): 29.
5. Ed Welch, "Depression's Odd Filter," CCEF, http://www.ccef .org/resources/blog/depression-s-odd-filter.
6. Brené Brown, "Listening to Shame," TED, March 2012, http:// www.ted.com/talks/brene_brown_listening_to_shame.
7. G. K. Chesterton, *Orthodoxy* (New York and London: John Lane Co., 1909), 223.
8. David Foster Wallace, *Infinite Jest* (New York: Back Bay Books, 1996), 77–78.

CHAPTER 6: I KISSED MARRIAGE HELLO AFTER KISSING DATING GOODBYE

1. Lewis Smedes, "Controlling the Unpredictable—The Power of Promising," *Christianity Today* 27:2 (January 21, 1983), 16–19.
2. Timothy J. Keller, "The First Wedding Day: Genesis 2:18–25," preached at Redeemer Presbyterian Church in Manhattan, New York, January 4, 2009.
3. Paige Benton, "Singled Out by God for Good," *Re-Generation Quarterly* (Summer 1997), http://ctlibrary/rq/1997/summer /3320.html.

4. Robert Murray McCheyne, *The Works of Rev. Robert Murrary McCheyne Complete in One Volume* (New York: Robert Carter & Brothers, 1874), 13.
5. C. S. Lewis, *Prince Caspian: The Return to Narnia* (New York: HarperCollins, 1951), 141.
6. Dave Harvey, *When Sinners Say "I Do,"* (City, PA: Shepherd Press, 2007).
7. Blaise Pascal, *Pensées*, # 377, rev. ed. (London: Penguin, 1995), 110.
8. Oscar Wilde, *The Critic as Artist* (New York: Mondial, 2007), 83.
9. Dick Keyes, *Beyond Identity: Finding Your Self in the Image and Character of God* (Ann Arbor, MI: Servant Books, 1984).
10. Gary Thomas, *The Sacred Search: What If It's Not About Who You Marry, But Why?* (Colorado Springs: David Cook, 2013), 66.

CHAPTER 7: WHERE FRIENDSHIP IS BORN

1. I believe this idea is from a conversation with Brené Brown and Oprah. Not exactly sure. Even less sure about sharing the fact that I occasionally watch *Oprah* and enjoy seeing people I love sitting on the couch with Oprah. I love Oprah. Mainly because I'll never forget her saying she is okay with the fact that she'll never lose weight because of her love for cheeseburgers. There's a sincere prayer in there somewhere. Probably just, "God, thank you for cheeseburgers. Amen."
2. Jon Acuff, *Stuff Christians Like* (Grand Rapids, MI: Zondervan, 2010), 243.
3. Chuck Klosterman, "Kobe Bryant Will Always Be an All-Star of Talking," *GQ* (March 2015), http://www.gq.com/sports/201503/kobe-bryant-nba-allstar?currentPage=2.
4. Timothy Keller with Kathy Keller, *The Meaning of Marriage: Facing the Complexities of Commitment with the Wisdom of God* (New York: Dutton, 2011), 104.

5. J. I. Packer, *Knowing God*, 20th anniversary ed. (Downers Grove, IL: InterVarsity Press, 1993), 41–42.
6. This idea is undoubtedly shaped by Tim Keller. See Justin Taylor, "Keller: Gospel-Centered Ministry," May 23, 2007, http://www.thegospelcoalition.org/blogs/justintaylor/2007/05/23/keller-gospel-centered-ministry/.
7. Chris Rock, from his standup special, "Bigger and Blacker," HBO, 1999, https://www.youtube.com/watch?v=Y54_AHO4CkM.
8. Timshel is the famous phrase from John Steinbeck's *East of Eden*. It's taken from Genesis 4:7 when God reasons with Cain before he kills Abel. It signifies the choice between good and evil.
9. C. S. Lewis, *The Four Loves* (New York: Harcourt Brace, 1960), 66.

CHAPTER 8: CALLING ALL INTROVERTS

1. The Myers-Briggs personality test assigns four letters from a list of eight to define personality: *E* or *I* (extroversion or introversion), *S* or *N* (sensing or intuition), *T* or *F* (thinking or feeling), *J* or *P* (judgment or perception).
2. "Our wisdom, insofar as it ought to be deemed true and solid wisdom, consists almost entirely of two parts: the knowledge of God and of ourselves. But as these are connected together by many ties, it is not easy to determine which of the two precedes and gives birth to the other. . . . Every person, therefore, on coming to the knowledge of himself, is not only urged to seek God, but is also led by the hand to find Him." John Calvin, *The Institutes of the Christian Religion*, trans. Henry Beveridge (Peabody, MA: Hendrickson Publishers, 2008), 4.
3. Frederick Buechner, *Wishful Thinking: A Seeker's ABC* (Woonsocket, R.I.: Mowbray, 1994), 118–19.
4. Susan Cain, "A Manifesto for Introverts," *Quiet* (New York: Random House, 2012, 2013), 264.

5. Adam S. McHugh, *Introverts in the Church* (Downers Grove, IL: InterVarsity Press, 2009), 185.
6. Eugene Peterson, *The Contemplative Pastor: Returning to the Art of Spiritual Direction* (Grand Rapids, MI: Wm. B. Eerdmans, 1989), 21.
7. C. S. Lewis, *Mere Christianity* (New York: Harper Collins, 1952), 51.
8. Edmund P. Clowney, "The Biblical Theology of the Church" in *The Church in the Bible and the World: An International Study,* ed. D. A. Carson (Eugene, OR: Wipf & Stock Publishers, 2002), 29.

CHAPTER 9: DONUTS ARE A WHOLE FOOD IF YOU TAKE OUT THE *W*

1. Wendell Berry, "Renewing Husbandry" in *The Way of Ignorance* (Emeryville, CA: Shoemaker & Hoard, 2005), 95.
2. G. K. Chesterton, *St. Francis of Assisi* (Garden City, NY, 1957), 16.
3. Tina Fey, *Bossypants* (New York: Little, Brown & Co., 2011), 115–18.

CHAPTER 10: TWEETING OURSELVES TO DEATH

1. For the life of me I can't find who originally said this on Twitter, but I am so thankful they did because it is painfully accurate.
2. Jonathan Franzen, "Liking Is for Cowards. Go for What Hurts," *New York Times,* May 28, 2011, http://www.nytimes .com/2011/05/29/opinion/29franzen.html?_r=0.
3. Jonathan Franzen, "What's Wrong with the Modern World," *The Guardian,* September 13, 2013.
4. Jaron Lanier, *You Are Not a Gadget* (New York: Vintage Books, 2011), xiii.
5. John Acuff (@JonAcuff) on Twitter, 7:48 p.m., September 6, 2013, https://twitter.com/jonacuff/status/376129906763390976.

6. Walter Brueggemann, *Spirituality of the Psalms* (Minneapolis, MN: Fortress Press, 2002).

7. Margaret Atwood, *Alias Grace* (New York: Anchor Books, 2007), 298.

8. David Foster Wallace, *Infinite Jest* (New York: Back Bay Books, 1996, 2006), 203.

CHAPTER 11: SIDE-HUGGING JESUS

1. John Updike uses this image in his short story, "Son" in *The Early Stories* (New York: Random House, 2003).

2. "God is too good to be unkind. He is too wise to be confused. If I cannot trace His hand, I can always trust His heart." Attributed to the British preacher Charles Spurgeon.

3. Marilynne Robinson, *Gilead* (New York: Picador, 2004), 114. I wish every Christian bookstore put a rack full of this book near the register instead of the latest hot take.

4. Flannery O'Connor, *The Habit of Being: Letters of Flannery O'Connor* (New York: Farrar, Strauss & Giroux, 1979, 1999), 354.

5. John Newton, "Prayers Answered by Crosses," *John Newton's Olney Hymns* (Minneapolis, MN: Curiosmith, 2011), 153.

6. C. S. Lewis, *The Magician's Nephew* (New York: HarperCollins, 1955), 152.

APPENDIX A

1. Seth Stevenson, "Don't Say Goodbye, Just Ghost," *Slate*, July 3, 2013, http://www.slate.com/articles/life/a_fine_whine/2013/07/ghosting_the_irish_goodbye_the_french_leave_stop_saying_goodbye_at_parties.html.

APPENDIX B

1. Brené Brown, *Daring Greatly* (New York: Gotham Books, 2012), 46.
2. Seth Godin, *Tribes: We Need You to Lead Us* (New York: Portfolio, 2008), 101.
3. C. S. Lewis, *Prince Caspian* (New York: HarperCollins, 1951, 1979), 233.

ABOUT THE AUTHOR

Sammy Rhodes is a campus minister with Reformed University Fellowship at the University of South Carolina. Rhodes is frequently invited to speak at conferences and churches on topics including anxiety and depression, approval, the Internet, pop culture, humor, theology, and leadership. Rhodes also has a popular Internet presence, which has been highlighted in *Huffington Post*, *Salon*, *Paste*, and *Christianity Today*.